D0058237

Library
Western Wyoming Community College

DISCARDED

THE GIFT OF TONGUES

The Gift of Tongues

~ TWENTY-FIVE YEARS
OF POETRY FROM
COPPER CANYON PRESS

*Edited and with an Introduction
by Sam Hamill*

COPPER CANYON PRESS

Copyright © 1996 by Copper Canyon Press

Publication of this book is supported by a grant from the Andrew W. Mellon Foundation. Additional support to Copper Canyon Press has been provided by the National Endowment for the Arts, the Lila Wallace–Reader's Digest Fund, the Lannan Foundation, and the Washington State Arts Commission. Copper Canyon Press is in residence with Centrum at Fort Worden State Park.

Special thanks to the following: To James Laughlin and New Directions for permission to reprint excerpts from Ezra Pound's *Confucius*; to White Pine Press for permission to reprint "The Gift of Tongues" from Sam Hamill's *Destination Zero*; and to George Tsutakawa for permission to use his wonderful copper mask as a cover image for this anthology.

Library of Congress Cataloging-in-Publication Data
The gift of tongues: twenty-five years of poetry from Copper Canyon Press / edited and with an introduction by Sam Hamill
p. cm.
Includes bibliographical references and index.
ISBN 1-55659-116-0 (CLOTH) / ISBN 1-55659-117-9 (PAPER)
1. Poetry – Collections. 2. American poetry – 20th century. 3. Poetry, Modern – 20th century – Translations into English.
1. Hamill, Sam.
PN6101.G64 1996
811'.5408 – DC20   96-25337

COPPER CANYON PRESS
P.O. BOX 271, PORT TOWNSEND, WASHINGTON 98368

EDITOR'S DEDICATION

To all those who contributed to this gift of poetry,
former and present staff and board members, contributors,
and to the poets:

Funny – I never could keep my mouth shut;
it gets worse the older I grow . . .

Too bad I was no help to the government
but they still pay me in old wine sacks.

– Su Tung-p'o

Library
Western Wyoming Community College

CONTENTS

A Personal Introduction

WHATEVER MY ASPIRATION OR INTENTIONS that bright, crisp November morning in 1972, Jim Gautney and I hauled the old galley press up three flights of tenement steps and installed it in our kitchen. The first snows had already fallen in the Rockies, and Denver was vivid with autumn leaves. The press and a small cabinet of type – enough to handset two pages of poetry at a time was purchased with the five hundred dollars I'd been awarded by the Coordinating Council of Literary Magazines "for producing the best college or university literary journal in the country" as editor of the University of California, Santa Barbara, journal *Spectrum.* I had a pat on the back, five hundred bucks in hand, and a 'fifty-four Ford panel truck that couldn't make the trek across the mountains when I decided to start a press. I was in no position to entertain dreams of great expectations.

I had made a commitment to poetry, to a life centered in poetry, when I had returned to college following four years in the Marine Corps in the early sixties. While "serving my country" in the occupied nation of Okinawa, I had begun Zen Buddhist practice and become a conscientious objector. Upon my return to the U.S. in 1964, I had given shelter to a battered woman, a woman without resources of any kind and whose life was very obviously at risk. I had also begun to address my own violence as a young man, and the misogynistic, racist culture I had experienced growing up in Utah in the forties and early fifties. I had become politicized by reading first the Beats, then *The Second Sex*, and by the civil rights and antiwar movements in which I was active even to the point of running for a seat in the California assembly on the Peace and Freedom Party ticket in 1968.

Like me, the woman I sheltered was a high school dropout. We married to take advantage of my G.I. school benefits. Our daughter was born in 1965, just weeks after my discharge from the Marine Corps. For a couple of years, I had struggled with lowest middle-class life: a car on credit while I worked as a bill collector in Los Angeles. But I was miserable. I dreamed of a writing life. My brief marriage collapsed almost exactly as I entered Los Angeles Valley College in 1966. She wanted middle-class stability. I wanted to find myself. I needed a *raison d'être*. An orphan myself, the most difficult decision I would ever make would be to leave my daughter, my only blood relative, to pursue my conviction that only through the writing life, and through Zen practice and social activism, could I learn to live with myself. It was almost a religious conversion. And a final rejection of middle-class values and a life on credit. My daughter, Eron, and I remained close and spent time together summers and on many holidays.

No doubt I reflected on all that and more as we wedged the press up the stairs groan by groan. And no doubt I reflected back on the jail cells in which I'd spent much of my adolescence while living the "Beat" life on the streets of San Francisco, Los Angeles, and in lockups in one-cow towns from Arizona to Montana. The study of poetry began to bring emotional discipline into my daily life as never before. It brought me face-to-face with my own history of violence and stupid, destructive relationships with women. The Press would expand that discipline in more ways than I could have imagined.

I had begun Ezra Pound studies at Los Angeles Valley College and continued under Hugh Kenner while at Santa Barbara, and was immersed in Confucius and the *Cantos*, so I no doubt perceived the establishment of the as yet unnamed press as following in a fugitive tradition. From Shelley to Whitman to Rexroth, poetry had demanded revolution from within. James Laughlin's work at New Directions certainly was one kind of model, as were any number of small-press editors and printers including Clifford Burke, Noel Young, and George Hitchcock. Whatever else I thought, I did not have ambitions or expectations beyond the desire to help a few young poets get some good work into print in small editions while pursuing my own Confucian studies and Zen practice.

I had been formally trained in some aspects of editing while studying journalism at Los Angeles Valley College where I edited both the student newspaper and the literary journal. But my editorial work at Copper Canyon Press would prove to be a vastly different undertaking. For the first fifteen or more years of the Press, I would not only be an unpaid editor, but as co-publisher with Tree Swenson, would have to find the means for paying for paper, printing, binding, and mailing bills, as well as other general overhead. Neither of us would derive a livable wage from the Press for nearly two decades, and I still do not. I would come to see my work as part of a gift to poetry. I felt then, and feel today, that my work as poet, as editor, translator, and critic is rooted in my conviction that poetry saved me from a lifetime of misery; poetry helped me find myself as only a lifelong commitment can; devotion to poetry came to mean an authentic search for a moral and disciplined life, a *kadō* or "way of poetry" not unlike that to which Saigyō, Bashō and other Zen poets ascribed. I wanted to make the gift the work of a lifetime. I sought a life of gratitude and revolutionary conviction. My commitment would be to the way of poetry, not to its sycophants or celebrities.

Gautney and I were joined shortly by Tree Swenson and Bill O'Daly, and through a dream of mine, Copper Canyon Press was born. My dream had returned me to childhood memories of watching the huge open-pit mine in Bingham, on the southwest corner of the Great Salt Lake Valley, slowly devour an entire mountain. The "copper canyon" of the northern Utes was a place for digging copper for medicine bracelets and such. The American genocide practiced against native cultures in the nineteenth century, I felt, left our nation morally impoverished and made the war in Vietnam inevitable. Copper being a low-grade

ore, and the place name reflecting ecological and spiritual values that are as an-
cient as the original people, we settled on our name.

Bill O'Daly had worked with me on *Spectrum*, and one of the young poets we
admired was Gerald Costanzo. Thus a chapbook of his poems, *Badlands*, would
become the first Copper Canyon Press title, issued in 1973, along with three more
titles including *The Berrypicker*, a first book by a young woman whose poetry
O'Daly and I had also championed at Santa Barbara, Marianne Wolfe. The edi-
tions were small, five hundred or fewer, and we had no real distribution but word
of mouth and a few stores or dealers specializing in poetry. Type was set by hand, a
master proof was pulled, and the pages were printed offset on a rackety, crotchety
Multilith 1000, an infernal machine I came to view as a karmic test, one of the final
circles of hell before a glimpse of paradise.

During the year and a half we spent in Denver, we all held day jobs, our editing
and typesetting and printing taking place nights and weekends. With Tree
Swenson's formal training in studio arts and her love of books, it was natural that
she would begin serious study in the art and history of the printed book. I fol-
lowed suit. With no formal training at the press or the type drawer, with each
book published, we learned lessons in production and typography. Her home-
work and devotion would eventually make her one of the best book designers in
the country, and would go a very long way toward establishing our credibility.

Bill O'Daly left the Press to marry and return to school in Fresno and graduate
school at Eastern Washington University. He would eventually devote seventeen
years to translating six volumes of later poetry by Pablo Neruda, books that would
be published by Copper Canyon Press and become our best-selling titles.

In the spring of 1974, we received an offer from Joseph F. Wheeler, director of
Centrum, a nonprofit arts programming organization in Port Townsend. His lit-
erary programs director, W. M. Ransom, had been editor at *West Coast Poetry Re-
view* and author of our fourth title, *Finding True North & Critter*. Ransom believed
that establishing a literary press-in-residence would be a valuable tool, not only
for the summer Port Townsend Poetry Symposium (as the Port Townsend Writ-
ers' Conference was then known), but also for high school workshops during the
winter. Centrum would have access to a working editor, and the Press and Cen-
trum would benefit mutually. We would have a no-rent building for the Press for
several years, then convert to low rent. Centrum would serve as a host and um-
brella organization to qualify the Press to apply for assistance from the National
Endowment for the Arts.

It was clear from the beginning that such a life would be labor-intensive rather
than capital-intensive publishing. It would mean poverty of all but spirit. We
made the move in the early spring of 1974. With the aid of Centrum, I had ob-
tained a Chandler & Price platen press and a little elementary instruction from

Tom Whitridge, who had conducted introductory letterpress printing workshops during the first Poetry Symposium. I would in turn teach Swenson, and the early reputation of the Press would be built around our dedication to the arts of the printed book as well as by editorial decisions.

The early years in Port Townsend were especially difficult. Swenson and I bought a parcel of land, cleared some space among the trees, and lived in a twenty-foot travel trailer without running water or electricity. I taught in artists-in-education programs and in prisons in Alaska, Washington, and California, spending much of every winter living in cheap motels. Meanwhile Swenson handled daily administration of the Press as well as designing and printing books. I read all manuscripts, as I do today, and worked on the press when home from teaching stints. When my daughter came to live with us to finish junior high and high school here, we moved into the bare shell of the small cabin I was building, living at first without interior walls or insulation, cooking and heating by wood stove, and hauling our water in five-gallon containers from the Press. I would continue my transitory life-by-begging-bowl through the 1980s, slowly building the house as we slowly built the Press, going to work each day to greet the day's tasks without benefit of regular income or health insurance, retirement plan or any of the other normal perquisites of middle-class life in America, but with a constant devotion to love's labors.

The Press began to receive funding from the National Endowment for the Arts in 1975, and for the remainder of the seventies, it would be, as James Laughlin once observed to my alternating consternation and delight, "a mom and pop operation." Swenson and I worked day and night and studied at home, huddled by the wood stove in kerosene light. My daughter and I built the next section of the house so she could have her own bedroom. Then, as now, I bucked wood for winter. Hard physical labor has always been a source of poetry for me, a source of self-worth. Even then, I did not have great aspirations or expectations. I expected to enjoy the work at hand. When mom and pop make a family out of expectation, they set themselves up for doom. Then as now, my work habits were rooted in elemental Zen. I get up and go to work because that's what I most love to do. *Laborare est orare.*

When a young editor introduced himself at our door to inquire as to whether we might let him use one of our presses sometime, we welcomed Scott Walker, and the Copper Canyon facility served as midwife to Graywolf Press, which Walker co-founded with Linda Foster as a small letterpress publisher. Years later, Swenson would become the book designer for Graywolf. Several young poets including Kim Stafford, Kathleene West, and Tim McNulty, among others, learned the rudiments of platen press printing and book design here, producing, with our help and direction, and assistance from the NEA, their own first books.

We were able to assist, in various ways, Sam and Sally Green at (then) Jawbone Press, now producing letterpressed limited edition books at Brooding Heron Press; Jim Bodeen and his Blue Begonia Press; Tom and Barbara Rea at Dooryard Press; Donnell Hunter and others have gone on to print books and chapbooks via letterpress, thanks to the generosity we were able to extend, courtesy of Centrum and the NEA. Swenson taught introductory letterpress printing workshops during the Poetry Symposium, her students learning to look at letter forms and language differently, while producing beautiful broadsides.

Our production during the seventies was at best haphazard, schedule determined in part by my availability, in part by our ability to pay for fine papers, lead type, and binding. But a book coming in from the bindery or the sewing of the first copy of a new chapbook was a momentous occasion. Some titles were designed and printed by Swenson; some were my work; most were collaborative. But each was met with great joy, only to be looked at again later with a cold and clinically critical eye.

But it soon became clear to us that we could not continue to produce our trade books on the letterpress without pricing ourselves out of the marketplace. The cost of materials ran too high, and electronic typesetting was making rapid advancements. In some cases, such as Kenneth Rexroth's *The Silver Swan* (1976), we issued a limited letterpressed edition commercially clothbound or handbound (early editions by John and Annie Hansen, later ones by Marsha Hollingsworth), then ran a photo-offset edition bound in paper for the trade. Other editions, such as Swenson's magnificent production of Denise Levertov's *Wanderer's Daysong* (1981) and equally elegant *Priest and a Dead Priestess Speaks* by H.D. (1983) were issued in hand-bound limited editions only. But such books are as much a work of art as a tool, and they quickly disappear into rare book collections.

For my part, the decision to abandon the limited edition as a primary form of publishing was made easy by my encounter with Carolyn Forché. Having won the Yale Younger Poets Award for her first book, Forché approached me with the manuscript of her second, *The Country Between Us*, declaring her love for Copper Canyon Press and especially for our commitment to other younger poets such as Olga Broumas, along with our political convictions. We agreed that I would design and print a two hundred copy edition to be letterpressed and handbound and signed by the poet, then produce both clothbound and paperbound editions for the trade. We shook hands on it, and I went to work on the press.

However, a month or two into production, I received a letter informing me that the poet had signed a contract with Harper and Row for a trade edition. Hard on its heels, I received an irate letter from the Academy of American Poets telling me that I was "ruining the Lamont Award," which Forché had won, by not making available a twelve hundred copy first edition, the purchase of which by the Academy was part of the award. The Academy, I was informed, would purchase its copies from the commercial edition. Harper and Row reproduced my design, as did Forché's English publisher, and the book went merrily on to fame and glory.

There are many good reasons for signed contracts, not least of which is one's friends. It took a long time for me to come to terms with treating my work here as a business transaction, to separate my personal commitments from professional ones. Editing is a labor of passion as well as of intelligence, but publishing for the trade, profitably or otherwise, is a business. As we began to develop a staff at the Press, the need for proper job descriptions and contracts with writers became essential.

The bitter pills were very few, offset by the boundless glee in discovering a David Lee, Milton scholar and pig farmer in Paragonah, Utah, and one of the most original voices in American poetry of the last twenty years, a poet with a vision and a body of work that is laudable. I read his first poems while we were still in Denver. "Discovering" and publishing new poets like Primus St. John, Gladys Cardiff, among many, and setting type by hand brought me far more deeply into their poetry , the work itself becoming a deep meditation on their poems.

Likewise my friendship with Olga Broumas dates from 1977, when she was giving readings as a Yale Younger Poet and I was receiving anonymous hate mail from certain feminist separatists who believed that a man, especially a reformed batterer, had no right to speak on behalf of feminism. Her faith in my struggle for right-mindfulness was and remains a blessing, and her poetry and her life have been a part of my life for nearly twenty years. Her breath is my breath.

The same may be said of the late great Thomas McGrath, with whom I became friends while I was at work on a book-length poem, *Triada*, in the mid-seventies. He was not at all well-published at the time. He was a wise counsel, a good friend and sometime editor, and being invited to edit and introduce his *Selected Poems* a decade later was an honor and a privilege. In Broumas and McGrath I found truly kindred spirits, poets whose body of work was rooted in moral convictions, determined and articulated by the poetry they read and wrote.

Looking back at the first ten years from this angle, I am particularly proud to have been editor for W.M. Ransom, Kathleene West, Robert Hedin, and many other young poets. Paul Hansen's wonderful poems from the Chinese, *Before Ten Thousand Peaks*, and Kenneth O. Hanson's translations of Han Yü, *Growing Old Alive*, initiated our long-standing commitment to Asian poetry in translation. As my own continuing study of Asian literature would reveal, there are threads that lead from Tu Fu, Li Po, and T'ao Ch'ien, on through Saigyō and Bashō, right up to Gary Snyder and Olga Broumas, Thomas Centolella, and Arthur Sze. American poetry was blossoming in part as a direct result of the introduction of Zen and other Asian literary traditions. The poets of the T'ang dynasty became models for the conduct of my own life.

The following decade was a period of growth and stabilization. Mary Jane Knecht, who had served an apprenticeship at the Press several years earlier, came on staff as a part-time employee in 1984. We mapped plans for better book promotion and administration, and added the Neruda series, Thomas McGrath, Carolyn Kizer, and Odysseas Elytis to a growing list. I continued to divide my time between the Press, prison, and public school workshops.

An NEA Writing fellowship in 1980 and a Guggenheim Fellowship in 1983 brought electricity and running water to the house. I felt for the first time in my life that the literary community did indeed value my poetry. Perhaps I make too much of what many say is a crapshoot, but I felt that the honors acknowledged a body of work made possible only through long, intense, and often painful self-assessment. Those fellowships were very important gifts not only because I desperately needed the money, but because I even more desperately needed to feel I'd earned a little respect as a poet, as a working artist. Maintaining an artistic life has informed my every duty as a working editor, from selection of manuscripts to the writing of jacket and catalogue copy.

Swenson and Knecht transformed Copper Canyon Press from a very good "mom and pop operation" into a working Press. Under-staffed and under-funded, the Press, principally through their diligence and dedication, would enter this decade as a nonprofit publisher with a working board of directors and a (however humbly) paid staff. No longer just the tool of love's labor for a couple of young aficionados, the Press had to meet all the responsibilities of publishing for the general trade in a very competitive marketplace. Neither money nor public appreciation can "repay" a gift that is made for its own sake. Tree Swenson and Mary Jane Knecht gave something enduring and noble to North American poetry, something very few can come to fully understand or properly appreciate, and their gifts continue out in ever-expanding circles to touch all those who read a book or listen to a poem they delivered to the world.

At a time when many other Presses were encouraged by the NEA and other arts organizations to broaden their scope to include publication of fiction and nonfiction, we renewed our commitment to publishing poetry exclusively, dividing our list among younger poets, major works projects, and poetry in translation. We established proper working order, attending to such necessities as publishing a book when it is scheduled to be published, making and sending out bound galleys for review, placing ads in appropriate journals, and preparing an annual catalogue of titles. And we laid the groundwork, including grant writing, that would make us fiscally responsible.

When Carolyn Kizer came to us, she came primarily, I believe, because of Swenson's reputation as a book designer and because our commitment is to poetry exclusively, and she knew she could help us while we helped her. With four highly successful titles published and more to follow, it has been a fruitful relationship. And her prose on poetry, *Proses*, published in 1993, became our first in the *Writing Re: Writing Series* of books on poetry by leading poets.

When Swenson and Knecht left the Press in 1993, Jennifer Pettit had already come on board as our second paid employee and became Associate Editor. Michael Wiegers left Coffee House Press in Minneapolis to become Managing Editor here. Janie Wilson was hired as Publisher, Kathleen Novello became our Bookkeeper, and John Berry became our Book Designer. The Board of Directors was expanded, and a grant from the Mellon Fund allowed us to bring in Peter Simpson as Development Director. In the summer of 1995, Jennifer Pettit left, and Carol Light joined the staff.

For the first time, more than twenty years after its founding, the Press had a reasonably complete staff. Not until the staff was filled out did I begin to realize just how often in those first twenty years we lived in a state approaching crisis. In retrospect, that three people were able to accomplish what we did staggers me. And for the fact that we are better organized than ever before, and because the gratification I feel at work each day is greater than ever before, I am indebted to old and new staff alike. Every book is still a mystery and a great delight, every task a pleasure. With a new and larger staff in place, we have increased production from six to ten titles per year, sponsored more public readings, and advanced the cause of poetry in general.

Although I had read Hayden Carruth's poetry for many years (his anthology, *The Voice That is Great Within Us* had been a handbook for a group of us at Santa Barbara in 1971), until he asked me to reissue *The Sleeping Beauty* and we began to talk, I had no idea of just how much of his work I had missed because it had been published in fugitive editions. His *Selected Poems* had come and gone with barely a notice. And thus his two volume award-winning *Collected Poems* was born. This is work of monumental importance, and to think of having had a hand in presenting it is enough to move me to tears.

It has also been a privilege to serve so many younger poets in recent years–far too many to list individually. So many books, each with its own intrigues, each with its own ongoing biography. But in the long view, simply this deep abiding pleasure, this gratitude really, for a life spent in the service of something greater than the never-ending American obsession with the search for immediate self-gratification.

I'm not interested in poetry movements and I've never tried to establish or organize a "school" of poetic thought around the Press. I have selected for publication poetry that has moved me, poetry that seems *memorable* to me in some way. My testing kit includes the sage advice of the third century writer Lu Chi whose

Wen Fu: The Art of Writing I translated fifteen years ago; it includes the *Ta Hsueh* or *Great Learning* of Confucius and Ezra Pound's notions of melopoeia, logopoeia, and phanopoeia, and the good sound common sense of *The* ABC *of Reading*; and it also contains a working bullshit detector perfected in the prison workshop and in thirty years of work on behalf of battered women and children; and an adult life spent as a conscientious objector, which is to say a contrarian, whose discipline is centered in the study and practice of poetry and Zen.

Lu Chi, writes in his famous preface to the *Wen Fu*:

> When studying the work of the Masters,
>   I watch the working of their minds.
> Surely, facility with language
>   and the charging of the word with energy
> are effects which can be achieved
>   by various means.
> Still, the beautiful can be distinguished
>   from the common, the good from the mediocre.
> Only through writing and then revising and revising
>   may one gain the necessary insight.
> We worry whether our ideas may fall short of their subjects,
>   whether form and content rhyme.
> This may be easy to know,
>   but it is difficult to put into practice...
> When cutting an axe handle with an axe,
>   surely the model is at hand....

The work of the poet, the work of the Zennist, is to follow the heart's truth. Nothing could be more difficult. Nothing could be more simple. Lu Chi "bolted the door and spent ten years on the classics." Five or six years of university education had prepared me for a lifetime of study. Zen practice and poetic practice become one; writing and editing and translating are one meditation.

Over the past thirty-five or forty years, American poetry has blossomed as never before. The Beat poets brought poetry out of the academy and into the streets and homes of educated blue-collar people and introduced it into various subcultures that evolved around jazz and theater as well as around literature. They reinvented the public poetry reading. The civil rights movement of the fifties and sixties helped introduce African-American poets such as Maya Angelou, Lucille Clifton, and Amiri Baraka to a growing white middle-class audience.

With the founding of the National Endowment for the Arts, American poetry was energized as never before. The NEA assisted dozens of small presses and hundreds of small journals that published the early poetry of Margaret Atwood, Susan Griffin, Robin Morgan, and many other vanguard feminist poets. Native American poets such as Simon Ortiz, Adrian Louis, and Joy Harjo, and Latin American and Asian American poets have reached international audiences through the gifts of labor at small presses surviving on minuscule (by trade publishing standards) budgets and seemingly inexhaustible devotion.

I was introduced to the Beat poets by James Laughlin's New Directions Publishing, a one-man "pop operation" responsible for my education in Pound, Williams, Rexroth, Levertov, Snyder, Lorca, Rimbaud, and dozens of others too numerous to mention. Ginsberg and other Beat poets came by way of Lawrence Ferlinghetti's City Lights Books. I had discovered W. S. Merwin and Charles Simic in the pages of George Hitchcock's remarkable *Kayak*; Atwood through small Canadian presses; Philip Levine through Unicorn Press; Robert Duncan, Jack Spicer and others through San Francisco presses; Jim Harrison through *Sumac*; Tom McGrath and Ivor Winters through Swallow Press.

By the early seventies, our poetry was becoming democratized, diverse as never before. Only a generation or two earlier, "American poetry" was basically a poetry rooted in the Latin and Greek every poet was expected to study; today, our poets are schooled in Chinese and Japanese poetry, in the oral traditions of African and Native American cultures, as well as in European traditions. The poetry of Rumi and Kabir and Mirabai are part of every poet's education. Most of our leading poets translate from at least one other language. And most of this essential work has come to us through small private or nonprofit presses.

For two decades, the NEA has brought poets to children's classrooms, put poetry on buses and bookstore shelves, and through small fellowships judged by fellow working artists, sent a message to our leading poets that their labors have lent something to our national character. The entire budget for the NEA has never exceeded our national budget for military marching bands. The city of Berlin routinely budgets more money for support for the arts than our national budget. Canadians invest six or seven times what we do, per capita, in public support for the arts. And of the entire NEA budget, support for poetry, for poets and for small presses was but one minuscule portion. And yet the return has been enormous. All over the world, the literati are going to school on poets as diverse as John Ashbery, Adrienne Rich, Lucille Clifton, Allen Ginsberg, W. S. Merwin, Hayden Carruth, Denise Levertov, et al. NEA support also encouraged private foundations to contribute and encouraged community involvement and local support as well.

I couldn't, in my wildest dream, imagine a world in which my small gift would be multiplied by so many generous hands. But that is exactly how the gift of poetry works: the gift of inspiration is transformed by the poet into a body of sound which in turn is given away so that it may inspire and inform another, who in turn adds to the gift and gives it away again. I have included a poem of my own, "The Gift of Tongues," as a title poem precisely because it addresses the phenomenon of the gift economy as it applies to poetry, and responds to that age-old question of what is "lost in translation" and what can be brought across the rivers of language.

Without the good faith and generosity of Centrum and the National Endowment for the Arts, Copper Canyon Press would probably still be issuing tiny editions for the specialty market. But the Press has become one of the major publishers of poetry in the past quarter century, currently publishing ten titles per year, ranging from Nobel Prize winners Odysseas Elytis, Pablo Neruda, Vicente Aleixandre, and Czeslaw Milosz, to leading feminist poets Olga Broumas, Susan Griffin, Jane Miller, Carolyn Kizer, and Shirley Kaufman. The Press also has done major works projects such as collected poems by Kay Boyle, Hayden Carruth, and W. S. Merwin, a groundbreaking program for poetry in translation, major selected editions by Thomas McGrath, David Bottoms, Eleanor Wilner, and others, and the occasional *Writing Re: Writing Series* volume, collecting prose on poetry by a prominent poet. And the Press continues to bring newly published poets to the national arena.

There is more great poetry being written and published in this country than ever before. I am convinced that a century or two hence, scholars and aficionados of poetry will come to view this period as a great flowering, perhaps the greatest since T'ang dynasty China. That the average citizen is unaware of the grace and generosity of this gift is unsurprising. Tu Fu, arguably China's greatest poet, was not discovered until nearly two hundred years after his death. Whitman published and promoted himself. Melville was a commercial failure. The first edition of *Prufrock* sold five hundred copies. Wallace Stevens's *Harmonium* was remaindered.

To those who say there are no poets of such magnitude today, I say, "Humbug!" Adrienne Rich is read in dozens of languages. Czeslaw Milosz is read all over the world. Allen Ginsberg has sold millions of books in dozens of languages. And this list could go on and on. When McGrath's *Selected Poems* was printed in Russian, his editor apologized for printing "only a puny 75,000" to sell to a pre-subscribed list. Furthermore, I refuse to measure poetry through any kind of popularity contest. As Odysseas Elytis once told me, "A real poet needs three readers. Since any poet worth his or her own salt has two intelligent friends, one spends a lifetime looking for the third reader."

The famous preface to the classic tenth century Japanese *Kokinshu* says it best: "Poetry begins in the heart." So what about the question of audience? The serious poet allows the poetry its own life. "Audience" is relative to what? From Dickinson's poetry without audience to Neruda's most bombastic public proclamations, the poetry finds its way.

Seamus Heaney has written, "In the case of heroes, it is not so much their procedures on the page which are influential as the composite image which has been projected on their conduct. That image, congruent with reality, features a poet tested by dangerous times. What is demanded is not any great public act of confrontation or submission, but rather a certain self-censorship, an agreement to forge, in the bad sense, the uncreated conscience of a race. Their resistance to this pressure is not initially or intentionally political, but there is of course a spin-off, a ripple effect, to their deviant artistic conduct. It is the refusal by this rear-guard minority which exposes to the majority the abjectness of their collapse, as they flee for security into whatever self-deceptions the party lines require of them. And it is because they effect this exposure that the poets become endangered: people are never grateful for being reminded of their moral cowardice."

All over the world there are brave souls who have been moved to face and eventually overcome their own moral cowardice through the moral imagination of a Hayden Carruth, a Tu Fu or an Adrienne Rich. A real poet *needs* three readers perhaps; but whether the poet finds an audience of dozens or hundreds or hundreds of thousands, the practice of poetry remains an act of solitary engagement with the world. It was just such a practice George Seferis sought when he wrote:

> I want no more than to speak simply, to be granted that grace.
> Because we've loaded even our songs with so much music that they're
>   slowly sinking
> and we've decorated our art so much that its features have been eaten
>   away by gold
> and it's time to say our few words because tomorrow the soul sets sail.

This sampling gathered from a quarter century of Copper Canyon Press is only evidence of a greater gift, one made possible through the generosity of the National Endowment for the Arts, Centrum, the Mellon Fund, the Lannan Foundation, the Lila Wallace–Readers Digest Fund, the Washington State Arts Commission, and other private and foundation donors. It is made possible by the hard invisible work of serious poets perfecting their craft in the long solitary hours and days of a lifetime. And by all those who have lent a hand and heart at Copper Canyon Press. But unless these gifts are given away in turn, they come to nothing. The best reading of a poem is aloud, before an audience of one or more educated listeners. Because only through the whole experience of the poem, including the giving away of the poem, can it work its whole magic. We provide the sheet music. The reader must bring breath, heartbeat, and voice to make the appropriate music.

Like theater and symphony and opera, the publication of poetry remains dependent upon patronage, as it has for thousands of years. This *anthologia* (from the Greek, meaning "flower-gathering of words") is but one bouquet. Copper Canyon is but one garden among several, each rich in diversity, including White Pine Press, BOA Editions, Coffee House Press, Curbstone Press, Graywolf Press, among others. Nothing is entirely self-originating, and Copper Canyon Press has flourished in part through mutual nourishment and through choosing cooperation over competition. Our future, like that of other nonprofit publishers, depends upon what we find in the begging bowl.

My greatest wish is that I not be the *only* editor at Copper Canyon Press, that we find some way to build an endowment so that the garden will continue to flourish long after my dust and ashes have been washed back into the roots by spring rains. For these flowers in hand, and for the lives and works of all the poets who give them, eternal gratitude. As Virgil says, *"Labor omnia vincit / Improbus et duris urgens in rebus egestus."* Roughly, "Only the work prevailed / and the stress of a lifetime of struggle."

– SAM HAMILL

THE GIFT OF TONGUES

Vicente Aleixandre

⌒ A LONGING FOR THE LIGHT [1985]

The Old Man Is Like Moses

Every man can be like that
and deliver the word and lift up his arms
and feel how the light sweeps
the old road dust from his face.

Because the sunset is over there.
Looking behind him: the dawn.
In front: the growing shadows. And the lights begin to shine!
And he swings his arms and speaks for the living
from inside his own death, all alone.

Because like Moses, he dies.
Not with the useless tablets and the chisel and the lightning in the mountains
but with words broken on the ground, his hair
of fire, his ears singed by the terrifying words.
And the breath is still in his eyes and the spark in his lungs
and his mouth full of light.

A sunset is sufficient for death.
A serving of shadow on the edge of the horizon.
A swarming of youth and hope and voices.
And in that place the generations to come, the earth: the borderline.
The thing the others will see.

Translated from the Spanish by Lewis Hyde

Heather Allen

In the Forest

Your step at once
More silent and more resonant,
Unmoving trees close ranks around you.
Darkness is suddenly deeper,
The web of light more clear.

Unseen the many eyes
That follow you, of sentinels
Stationed just beyond the rim
Of the senses, who merge into leaves and stillness
Just as you turn.

Shadow and substance, trees and light
Are finely braided here,
And passages to interwoven worlds
Are everywhere:
A flash of wings

From deep within
The coiled circuits of leaves,
The grey hush of the goshawk
Gliding suddenly from the weave,
Or a placeless echo of the owl's dream.

Like the cipher
Of a still impenetrable text,
Tracks mark the fragment of a path
Along the boundary of dawn
Or a night's hunting,

Into a world old maps describe
Only as "Forest," "Unexplored."

Composed and watchful, the trees
Surround a trove of secret lives
That seem unreachable to us –

Concentric rings
Of deer in the clearings, the phantom lynx
Poised in the dark of a pool,
The deep and humid dens
Of fox and owl,

And surreptitious, snaking roots that hold
The forest in miniature –
Spiral ferns and intricately threaded mosses,
The strands, invisible in shadow,
Of the spider's lair.

There, a drift of feathers
Cast up by the throes of night
Echoes a bird's last cry,
In the grip of something
Stealthy, huge-eyed, a darkness

Shaped by scent, and hearing
Tuned to the faintest heartbeat –
The slow, implacable pulse
Of the hunter,
The wild throbbing of his prey.

Dense with portents,
It is a labyrinth
Of furtive curves
And endless branching,
Barrier and entrance –

Still, as it is for the hero
In the forest of dream and legend
A place of trials and revelation.
You go there alone.
You must find your own way in.

Edgar Anawrok

⌒ IN THE DREAMLIGHT (TWENTY-ONE ALASKAN WRITERS) [1984]

Each Time

Each time
I visit you
it gets harder
to sit next to you
my hands want to
touchtouchtouch

I want you
like owls want eyes

John Balaban

Riding Westward

"Hence is't, that I am carryed towards the West
This day, when my Soules forme bends towards the East."
– John Donne, "Goodfriday, 1613. Riding Westward"

You know that something's not quite right.
Perhaps the town is one of those
on a water tower stuck up on a hill.
Or maybe the hill itself declares the name
in whitewashed stones set just behind the town.
The big thing is the grain elevators.
The blacktop runs straight to them
just as country roads point to steeples
in Protestant towns along the Rhine.
But these tall towers are filled with wheat,
with corn and oats and rye, not hymns
to the stern father who sends us to the fields
or bids us read his Book before we eat,
who shuts our eyes in calms of beast-like sleep.

This poem is no tract for Jesus.
No fewer evils or epiphanies of joy
rise up here than did in Europe, which these
good farmers left because it was a grave.
Still one wonders. What was all this for,
the grizzled duffer in the John Deere cap asks
as he shuffles to Main Street's secondhand sale.
Rubble of shoes in cardboard boxes. And boots,
old button boots, a pile of iron peaveys
which rolled cottonwoods down from the rivers,
the forest long since cleared. Cracked photos
of a jackrabbit hunt, the creatures piled high
in heaps before the log-and-sod schoolhouse.

I mean, he asks, as he tweaks his balls
through the hole in his right jean pocket,
why did they do this? What was it for?
The doves perch on a wire above the dusty road.
Swallows sweep into a storefront eave.
A clump of orange lilies closes with the day.
A CB chatters in a parked Ford truck
its back-bed loaded up with bales of hay:
"We got a Kojak takin' pictures
. . . he done a flipflop on the superslab."
The pickup's empty; the owner's in the bar.

The rightest place to worry this thing out
is at the first dead farmhouse outside town.
Sit there on the stoop's blistered boards
as swallows chitter towards their roosts,
the fat sun sinking in reddish pollen haze
beyond the silos, beyond the tasseled fields.

⌒ NEW & SELECTED POEMS [1997]

After Our War

After our war, the dismembered bits
– all those pierced eyes, ears slivers, jaw splinters,
gouged lips, odd tibias, skin flaps, and toes –
came squinting, wobbling, jabbering back.
The genitals, of course, were the most bizarre,
inching along roads like glowworms and slugs.
The living wanted them back but good as new.
The dead, of course, had no use for them.
And the ghosts, the tens of thousands of abandoned souls
who had appeared like swamp fog in the city streets,
on the evening altars, and on doorsills of cratered homes,
also had no use for the scraps and bits
because, in their opinion, they looked good without them.
Since all things naturally return to their source,
these snags and tatters arrived, with immigrant uncertainty,

in the United States. It was almost home.
So, now, one can sometimes see a friend or a famous man talking
with an extra pair of lips glued and yammering on his cheek,
and this is why handshakes are often unpleasant,
why it is better, sometimes, not to look another in the eye,
why, at your daughter's breast thickens a hard keloidal scar.
After the war, with such Cheshire cats grinning in our trees,
will the ancient tales still tell us new truths?
Will the myriad world surrender new metaphor?
After our war, how will love speak?

Anna Akhmatova Spends the Night on Miami Beach

Well, her book, anyway. The Kunitz volume
left lying on a bench, the pages
a bit puffy by morning, flushed with dew,
riffled by sea breeze, scratchy with sand
– the paperback with the 1930's photo
showing her in spangled caftan, its back cover
calling her "star of the St. Petersburg circle
of Pasternak, Mandelstam, and Blok,
surviving the Revolution and two World Wars."

So she'd been through worse . . .
the months outside Lefortovo prison
waiting for a son who was already dead, watching
women stagger and reel with news of executions,
one mother demanding, "Can you write about this?"
Akhmatova answered, "Yes."

If music lured her off the sandy bench
to the clubs where men were kissing
that wouldn't have bothered her much
nor the vamps sashaying in leather.

The decadence amid art deco fit nicely
with her black dress, chopped hair, and Chanel cap.

What killed her was the talk, the emptiness in the eyes
which made her long for the one person in ten thousand
who could say her name in Russian,
who could take her home, giving her a place
between Auden and Apollinaire
to whom she could describe her night's excursion
amid the loud hilarities, the trivial hungers
at the end of the American century.

Erin Belieu

⁓ INFANTA [1995]

Rondeau at the Train Stop

It bothers me: the genital smell of the bay
drifting toward me on the T stop, the train
circling the city like a dingy, year-round
Christmas display. The Puritans were right! Sin
is everywhere in Massachusetts, hell-bound

in the population. It bothers me
because it's summer now and sticky – no rain
to cool things down; heat like a wound
that will not close. Too hot, these shameful
percolations of the body that bloom
between strangers on a train. It bothers me

now that I'm alone and singles foam
around the city, bothered by the lather, the rings
of sweat. Know this bay's a watery animal, hind-end
perpetually raised: a wanting posture, pain
so apparent, wanting so much that it bothers me.

Marvin Bell

⌒ IRIS OF CREATION [1990]

A Primer about the Flag

Or certain ones. There are Bed & Breakfast flags.
They fly over vacancies, but seldom
above full houses. Shipboard, the bridge can say
an alphabet of flags. There are State flags
and State Fair flags, there are beautiful flags
and enemy flags. Enemy flags are not supposed
to be beautiful, or long-lasting. There are flags
on the moon, flags in cemeteries, costume flags.
There are little flags that come from the barrel
of a gun and say, "Bang." If you want to have
a parade, you usually have to have a flag
for people to line up behind. Few would
line up behind a small tree, for example,
if you carried it at your waist just like a flag
but didn't first tell people what it stood for.

⌒ THE BOOK OF THE DEAD MAN [1994]

The Book of the Dead Man #1

1. ABOUT THE DEAD MAN

The dead man thinks he is alive when he sees blood in his stool.
Seeing blood in his stool, the dead man thinks he is alive.
He thinks himself alive because he has no future.
Isn't that the way it always was, the way of life?
Now, as in life, he can call to people who will not answer.
Life looks like a white desert, a blaze of today in which nothing distinct can be
     made out, seen.
To the dead man, guilt and fear are indistinguishable.

The dead man cannot make out the spider at the center of its web.
He cannot see the eyelets in his shoes and so wears them unlaced.
He reads the large type and skips the fine print.
His vision surrounds a single tree, lost as he is in a forest.
From his porcelain living quarters, he looks out at a fiery plain.
His face is pressed against a frameless window.
Unable to look inside, unwilling to look outside, the man who is dead is like
    a useless gift in its box waiting.
It will have its yearly anniversary, but it would be wrong to call it a holiday.

2. More About the Dead Man

The dead man can balance a glass of water on his head without trembling.
He awaits the autopsy on the body discovered on the beach beneath the cliff.
Whatever passes through the dead man's mouth is expressed.
Everything that enters his mouth comes out of it.
He is willing to be diagnosed, as long as it won't disturb his future.
Stretched out, he snaps back like elastic.
Rolled over, he is still right-side-up.
When there is no good or bad, no useful or useless, no up, no down, no right way,
    no perfection, then okay it's not necessary that there be direction: up is down.
The dead man has the rest of his life to wait for color.
He finally has a bird's-eye view of the white hot sun.
He finally has a complete sentence, from his head to his feet.
He is, say, America, but he will soon be, say, Europe.
It will be necessary merely to cross the ocean and pop up in the new land, and
    the dead man doesn't need to swim.
It's the next best thing to talking to people in person.

⁓ ARDOR: THE BOOK OF THE DEAD MAN, VOL. 2 [1998]

The Book of the Dead Man #43

1. About the Dead Man and Desire

When the dead man itches, he thinks he has picked up a splinter.
Unable to free himself of an itch, the dead man thinks he has a splinter.
The dead man looks at a praying mantis and sees a pair of tweezers.

He offers himself to be walked on by claws.

He waits for the odd fox to trot across his chest and strings of ants to scrape him
pore to pore.

He anticipates the flaying action of chemicals and the sponge baths of the rain.

The dead man, scoured, is the ruby servant of the vineyard.

The dead man is the salt of the earth, the dust and the sawdust, the honey in the
wine.

Hence, his thoughts must rise to the moon and beyond to take his mind from
that splinter if it is a splinter, that itch if an itch is what it is.

Everything the dead man thinks has its other side.

The dead man thinks Saturn has been much married but forever lonely.

2. MORE ABOUT THE DEAD MAN AND DESIRE

If he were just valves and glue, just honey and chocolate, just hot and cold, the
dead man's thoughts would not hop, skip and jump so.

If he were just comparative, if he were absolute, if he knew his own mind, the
dead man's heart would not race so.

Who but the dead man wonders which of its moons Jupiter favors?

Who knows better than the dead man in his bones the pitch at which the earth
breathes?

The dead man is rapt before the altar of consciousness.

He enters the forbidden realms of experience without penalty.

To the dead man, there is something grave about umbrellas, something sinister
about servitude, something debilitating about knowledge – like sunlight on
slugs.

The dead man rolls back into place the rock that was moved to find out.

Like Sisyphus, the dead man wants what he has.

When there is no more meek, no vainglorious, no catch-as-catch-can, no inherit-
ance, no opportunity knocking that is not also the wind, then naturally the
dead man lives for love.

The dead man, fervent to feel, makes no distinction between a splinter and a
stinger that cost something its life.

Nelson Bentley

Iron Man of the Hoh

A mile at sea, Cake Rock, against the blue,
Lifts its seafowl sanctuary. Harsh squawks
float from the monoliths. A few
High breakers begin their crests and churns,
As I watch the sun sinking toward sea stacks,
And the world turns.

Again I've walked this tideline near La Push
From the Quillayute River to Hole In The Wall.
Offshore the rocks, like gods, stand fresh,
Unshaken by all the ocean's worst in storms,
And the world turns.

A dozen times I've walked it with Applebaum,
Painter and raconteur. One time he told
Me, with his monolithic aplomb,
As we strode along on shells and fish skeletons,
The story of the Iron Man of the Hoh:
And the world turns

On such accounts. It seems this Northwest Samson
Carried an iron cookstove twenty miles
Up the Hoh on his back, having
Homesteaded among Douglas firs, moss and ferns
In 1890. And as God made little apples,
And the world turns,

Two loggers, who saw him trotting the stove through the wood,
Asked, "Isn't that heavy?" He said, "No, but it's hard
To keep my balance on a log
When the sack of flour shifts in the oven."

So he raised his family far from any road;
And the world turns.

This man, John Huelsdonk, killed 300 cougars,
Once had his leg lacerated by a bear,
Crawled home two miles through firs and cedars,
And then walked forty miles into Forks.
His daughter pulled two men out of the Hoh by their hair;
And the world turns.

My wife and daughter, at the tidal edge,
Move by Cake Rock, which now, against the sun,
Goes purple-brown with the light's change,
Their pockets full of agates and odd stones.
My campfire gives the wind a pungent stain.
And the world turns.

Well, I've seen Babe Ruth hit two home runs
At Navin field, Frost at seventy-five,
Auden juggling the concerns
Of his century, Thomas in two taverns,
And Roethke, one of the giants of the alive;
And the world turns

Into legend. I remember Jean Garrigue
Embracing a Douglas fir in the Rain Forest.
Applebaum has fished among
Those basalt giants on which the seagull mourns.
Is that you, John Huelsdonk, where the breakers start?
And the world turns

Purple-blue in dusk. I think of how
My parents loved, imagined, and endured.
I gather wood and watch gulls float
On gathering breakers and settle on the crags.
The sun enters the ocean, a ball of blood,
And the world turns.

Berg, Stephen

⁓ CROW WITH NO MOUTH: IKKYŪ [1989]

ten fussy days running this temple all red tape
look me up if you want to in the bar whorehouse fish market

    *

no walls no roof no anything my house
doesn't get wet doesn't get blown down

    *

nature's a killer I won't sing to it
I hold my breath and listen to the dead singing under the grass

    *

a woman is enlightenment when you're with her and the red thread
of both your passions flares inside you and you see

    *

for us no difference between reading eating singing
making love not one thing or the other

On This Side of the River

To MILLIE

> *Simply trust:*
> *don't the petals also flutter down*
> *just like that?*
>   *– Issa*

I undress and lie down next to you in bed
and throw one of my legs across yours, I wait
until you are completely lost
then slide my head on the pillow with yours.
Your hair gets caught in my teeth.
I stretch a little to rub my head against yours, so
gently neither of us can feel it,
my breath goes and returns with yours.
There is a moon. Clouds streak its face.
At this late hour by the river the cherry trees stand alone,
black tongueless sentinels
that report nothing.
Wind shakes the flowers that hang over the water,
on the other side families sit down to eat.
I know it.
Not one petal has been torn loose,
and I lie here with my hands on you, not moving,
seeing us today under the trees
sitting with our legs crossed facing each other, talking,
and try to remember what we said.
Get up. I want you to explain
what no couple has ever understood–
the silence, our two skins, the fact that one dies first.
One angry face the color of the
blossoms flashes up and leaves.
The moon pours in. I begin telling you about
my life like the cabdriver in the story
who plows all night through Moscow desperate
for someone to listen to him and winds up at dawn

standing under a streetlamp, snow chilling his mouth,
telling his horse how terrible life is because his
five-year-old son died yesterday, and not one passenger would listen,
pulling the nag's ear down to his mouth, whispering deep
into it his unbearable story.

Alone

No one can hurt me. They've tried to kill me
so many times that nobody scares me now.
I know what kind of people want me dead:
fanatics in love, political, dressed up to look poor.
Nothing they can do is hidden from me.
This ordinary room of mine
is Paradise, cut off, a stone box
that overlooks my old street, people I used to know.
There's so little in it – two chairs,
bed, table, books, a red Persian prayer rug
with a cross in a golden field in the middle.
It could be called a trap; maybe it is.
But what I feel
is gratitude – to those who put me here
and, in their way, hung doors, cemented brick, glazed windows;
may they never be ill or worried; may life pass them by.
I'm up this morning with the workers, I see
my face in the streaked mirror, bleached with anxiety,
and what I am is what the sun is –
itself free of itself daily
even when its last shard of light eases under the rim of the earth.
Everything's dark. Whenever I shut my eyes.
I look outside; turn back;
look in the mirror and see
the small window, reflected:
pines miles away across a field,
a road, one cloud, clumps of bluish mist, some dead machine
slouched in a gown of rust – nature, things dropping back to nature,
me noticing my face among it all.
I tie one short ribbon in my gray hair
and step back – so much younger than the face I see –
nowhere, homeless, peaceful,

and speak to the voice inside me that answers me.
Sometimes I only sit here. Winds from a frozen sea
come through the open window. I don't get up, I
don't close it. I let the air touch me. I begin to freeze.
Twilight or dawn, the same pink streaks of cloud.

A dove pecks wheat from my extended hand,
those infinite, blind pages, stacked on my table . . .

some desolate urge lifts my right hand, guides me.
Much much older than I am, it comes down,
easy as an eyelid, godless, and I write.

⁓ THE STEEL CRICKET: VERSIONS, 1958–1996 [1997]

Clouded Sky

after Miklos Radnoti, June 8, 1940

The moon hangs on a clouded sky.
I am surprised that I live.
Anxiously and with great care, death looks for us
and those it finds are all terribly white.

Sometimes a year looks back and howls
then it drops to its knees.
Autumn is too much for me. It waits again
and winter waits with its dull pain.

The forest bleeds. The hours bleed.
Time spins overhead
and the wind scrawls
big dark numbers on the snow.

But I am still here
and I know why and why the air feels heavy –
a warm silence full of tiny noises circles me
just as it was before my birth.

I stop at the foot of a tree.
Its leaves cry with anger.
A branch reaches down. Is it strangling me?
I am not a coward. I am not weak, I am

tired. And silent. And the branch
is also mute and afraid as it enters my hair.
I should forget it, but I
forget nothing.

Clouds pour across the moon. Anger
leaves a poisonous dark green bruise on the sky.
I roll myself a cigarette,
slowly, carefully. I live.

*Translated from the Hungarian by Stephen Berg, F. J. Marks, and
Steven Polgar*

Orpingalik's My Breath: Eskimo Song

I have to sing
a song about myself
sick since autumn
stretched out in bed
weak as a child

I'm so sad
I wish my woman
lived with another man
in the house of someone
who'd protect her a man
hard and strong as winter ice

once I could track down anything
white bear caribou seal I can still see
myself on foot beating the men in kayaks
the white bear threw me down but I stabbed it
the seal I thought got away I hooked it

now dawn after dawn rolls by
and I'm still sick
the lamp's cold

I'm so sad I
wish she'd go away
to a better man
so weak I can't even
get up out of bed

who knows what can happen to a man
I lie here drained unable to rise
remembering how I beat everyone
to this kill or that
and they all stood there
with nothing

no oil for the lamp
only my memories are strong

David Bottoms

~ ARMORED HEARTS: SELECTED AND NEW POEMS [1995]

Under the Vulture-Tree

We have all seen them circling pastures,
have looked up from the mouth of a barn, a pine clearing,
the fences of our own backyards, and have stood
amazed by the one slow wing beat, the endless dihedral drift.
But I had never seen so many so close, hundreds,
every limb of the dead oak feathered black,

and I cut the engine, let the river grab the jon boat
and pull it toward the tree.
The black leaves shined, the pink fruit blossomed
red, ugly as a human heart.
Then, as I passed under their dream, I saw for the first time
its soft countenance, the raw fleshy jowls
wrinkled and generous, like the faces of the very old
who have grown to empathize with everything.

And I drifted away from them, slow, on the pull of the river,
reluctant, looking back at their roost,
calling them what I'd never called them, what they are,
those dwarfed transfiguring angels,
who flock to the side of the poisoned fox, the mud turtle
crushed on the shoulder of the road,
who pray over the leaf-graves of the anonymous lost,
with mercy enough to consume us all and give us wings.

Sierra Bear

One morning in June above Yosemite Valley, John Muir learned
the "right manners of the wilderness."
Walking out to sketch from the top of North Dome,
he followed his borrowed St. Bernard
to the edge of a meadow
and encountered, he says, his "first Sierra bear."

I like to picture that study in nature – artist and dog
poised in amazement at the heavy muscling,
the cinnamon elegance of pelt.
So easy to imagine the bear's huge grace –
sharp snout nuzzling air,
the small ears
twitching – you can almost understand an urge
to watch him run.
                              Here I smile at the eyes
of the bear as Muir, recalling
a rumor of shyness, "made a rush on him,
throwing up my arms, and shouting,"

and at Muir himself wincing as we all have
at our rude behavior. "As he held his ground
in a fighting attitude,
my mistake was monstrously plain."

Confused bear cocked back on a haunch,
artist's blundering arms frozen toward embrace –
what pardon these moments become
when the bear wades off through the lilies and grass.

Chinese Dragons

What do we want to give each other as we park under the sign
of the Electric Dragon?
Mysterious, you say, a name
like some bizarre arrangement of stars, a tail
of fire crawling all the way from China.

And tonight, looking up through the windshield
of my truck, we know already
what they'll be, no need to study the walls
of patterns, the yellow parrots
climbing stalks of cane, the rosebuds
unfolding under the paws
of red leopards, the erotic fish.

Hum of the needle, and that pale moment
of no turning back –
your eyes cut from mine
to the blue hand pointing toward the chair.

And when you sit in that chair, your blouse draped
on one shoulder, I know what claws out
of the sky and into your arm, what
will claw into my calf
and ankle, is something more than legend.

In your eyes as he needles the fire –
our desire for permanence and the permanence
of our desire.

Kay Boyle

⌒ COLLECTED POEMS [1991]

Ode to a Maintenance Man and His Family

Renato O. Jones, you maintain my beliefs
And service my thoughts when they cease to function.
You repair the ailing equipage of the present, transform
The past into flowers around the shuffle-board court
Where there were none before. You speak
The melodious languages of countries that bask
In the sun, employ vacuum respirator as though
It were rod or staff from the garden of Paradise.

You anoint windowpanes with Windex and kneel
In concern for stains on the carpeting,
As men knelt in ancient cathedrals where their voices
Murmured in prayer. You restore me with dance-steps
From harbors you knew: Shanghai, Marseilles, Trinidad,
And how many others. The songs that you sing
(As you unclog drains or retrieve lights when bulbs
flicker and fail, or weave copper patches into the webs
Of damaged screen doors) are magical with the music
Of names of your family: Carmelita, Christopher, Dissere,
Alex and Mark, and Kevin and Kenneth and Kerwin.

Each day you say to me – not in words but in the eloquence
Of your presence – that infinite patience with mankind is everything.

Robert Bringhurst

⁓ THE BEAUTY OF THE WEAPONS [1985]

The Song of Ptahhotep

FOR GEORGE PAYERLE

Good speech is rarer than jade. It is rarer
than greenstone, yet may be found among girls
at the grindstones, found among shepherds
alone in the hills.
I know how a man might speak to his grandson;
I cannot teach him to speak to the young women.

Still, I have seen at the well how the words
tune the heart, how they make one who hears them
a master of hearing. If hearing enters the hearer,
the hearer turns into a listener. Hearing is better
than anything else. It cleanses the will.

I have seen in the hills how the heart chooses.
The fists of the heart hold the gates of the ears.
If a grandson can hear his grandfather's words,
the words decades later
may rise like smoke from his heart
as he waits on a mountain and thinks of old age.

In the cave of the ear, the bones, like stars
at the solstice, sit upright and still,
listening in on the air as the muscle and blood
listen in on the skeleton.
Tongues and breasts of the unseen
creatures of the air
slither over the bones in the toothless
mouths of the ears.
To hear is to honor the sleeping snail
in the winter woodbox back of the forge.

You will see the new governor's ears
fill like pockets, his eyes
swell up with the easily seen,
yet his face is a dumped jug. His bones
wrinkle like bent flutes, his heart
sets and triggers like a beggar's hand.
The new governor's words are orderly, clean,
inexhaustible, and cannot be told
one from another, like funerals, like sand.

I have done what I could in my own time in office.
The river rises, the river goes down.
I have seen sunlight nest on the water.
I have seen darkness
puddle like oil in the palm of my hand.

Speak to your grandson by saying,
good speech is rarer than jade, it is rarer
than greenstone, yet may be found among girls
at the grindstones, found among shepherds
alone in the hills.
The heart is an animal. Learn where it leads.
Know its gait as it breaks. Know its range,
how it mates and feeds.
If they shear your heart bald like a goat, the coat
will grow back, though your heart may shudder from cold.
If they skin out your heart,
it will dry in your throat like a fish in the wind.

Speak to your grandson by saying,
my grandson, the caves of the air
glitter with hoofmarks
left by the creatures
you have summoned there.

My grandson, my grandson,
good speech is rarer than jade, it is rarer
than greenstone, yet may be found among girls
at the grindstones, found among shepherds
alone in the hills. The heart is a boat.

If it will not float, if it have no keel,
if it have no ballast, if it have
neither pole nor paddle nor mast,
there is no means by which you can cross.

Speak to your grandson by saying,
my grandson, the wake of the heart
is as wide as the river,
the drift of the heart is as long as the wind
and as strong as the rudder that glides through your hand.

Speak to your grandson by saying,
good speech is rarer than jade, it is rarer
than greenstone, yet may be found among girls
at the grindstones, found among shepherds
alone in the hills.
The fists of the heart as they open and close
on the rope of the blood in the well of the air
smell of the river.
The heart is two feet and the heart is two hands.
The ears of the blood hear it clapping and walking;
the eyes of the bones see the blooded footprints
it leaves in its path.

Speak to your grandson by saying,
my grandson, set your ear
on the heart's path,
kneeling there in honor
of the sleeping snail.

Parśvanatha

What is whole has no face. What
is apart from the whole has no body.

Yet somehow it is, and it is
manysided. Somehow it isn't
and is manysided. Somehow
it is manysided and isn't
and is. It cannot be touched
by the mind or by language, but somehow,
in spite of our thinking and talking,
it is, and in spite of our thinking
and talking, it isn't. Beyond
all our thinking and talking,
it isn't and is. This
is a map of our knowing. Own
nothing. Like breath in your lungs,
the truth passes through you.
Where space, motion and rest
come together is being. Where being
is tainted by death, you find
matter. Like water through cloth,
the unbroken plasma of action
drains through your bones.
What you are will be spelled by whatever
lies trapped in your hand.

On the fenceposts the heads of your
hungerless brothers are singing.

Olga Broumas

⁓ SOIE SAUVAGE [1979]

Oregon Landscape with Lost Lover

I take my bike
and ride down to the river
and put my feet into the water
and watch the ten toes play distortions

with the light. I had forgotten all this time
how good it is to sit by water
in sun all day and never have to leave
the river moving

as no lover ever moved
widehipped deadsure and delicate –
after a while I cannot bear
to look. Pleasure dilates me

open as a trellis
free of its green sharp glossy leaves like tongues
made out of mirrors gossiping
in the sun the wind. By which

I mean
somehow
free of the self.
Through all the hungry-eyed

criss-crossing slits along the trellis
finding them leaving them
bare and clean the widehipped delicate
green river flows

voluptuous as any lover anywhere
has been.

If I Yes

To be carried
Good luck of skin
Charmed roadside noise
Not to be plucked

Turn to me
As crows turn in midflight
And sketch an ocean
Over that curve of shoulder

With your eye
Sheer luck in Aries
Rebellious mellifluous
Insist on taking out the thorn

Let me be carried
Ribbonlike from your tongue
As if by language
Fabulous

A fathomless interruption
For it is both a tingling and a light
The difference is feeling
The simultaneous inscribe the soul

It will become very quiet
Encourage it
You have an eloquent tongue
Thrum it and it will leap

To its massive shudder
What the exterior beckons
Shape note singing precise plant
Starlight and the mountainous

Psalm grow-up-quick-of-butterfly
Colored wing-spreading eye
A noise cracks and creaks and is a nonsense
A noise is a nonsense cracks and creaks

Glossed shadow mental stills tarot
Black on black lake on lake marble marble
Of women saturated and rich
I have never seen you so happy and

It was good seeing you
My shells, my shy girls
Give me a shadow touch me with light
The dream of my life is to throw myself

The color of Warhol's people
I want to eat my life
Beauty monument design
If I'm not up by 11:30 don't wake me

~ PERPETUA [1989]

Touched

                    Cold
December nights I'd go
and lie down in the shallows
and breathe the brackish tide till light

broke me from dream. Days I kept busy
with fractured angels' client masquerades.
One had a tumor
recently removed, the scar

a zipper down his skull, his neck
a corset laced with suture.
I held, and did my tricks, two
palms, ten fingers, each a mouth

suctioning off the untold harm
parsed with the body's violent grief
at being cut. Later a woman
whose teenage children passed on in a crash

let me massage her deathmask
belly till the stretch
marks gleamed again, pearls
on a blushing rise. A nurse of women HIV

positives in the City
came, her strong young body filled
my hands. Fear grips her only
late at night, at home, her job

a risk on TV. It was calm, my palm
on her belly and her heart
said Breathe. I did. Her smile
could feed. Nights I'd go down

again and lie down on the gritty
shale and breathe the earth's salt
tears till the sun
stole me from sleep and when you

died I didn't
weep nor dream but knew you
like a god breathe in
each healing we begin.

Olga Broumas & T Begley

Sappho's Gymnasium

Outside memory worship never dies

That wish to embrace the great poplar

I woke and my bed was gleaming

Trees fill my heart

Torn mist doves I will love

Light struts cannot be broken

Make praise populations will last

            *

"I have a young girl good as blossoming gold
her ephemeral face I have formed of a key
dearer than skylark homelands"

A full twelve hours like a toiler like Lorca
archaic to bone we parse lark grove

Dutyfree dove seapitched Eleni
nectar your carafe seafounder

Preumbilical eros preclassical brain

*

Blueprint I have hearing over knife
prime workshop these forests verbed by breezes

Horizon helicoptera
Lesbian your cups

Hermaphrodyte phototaxis

*

Limblooser sweetbitter's scale holds the hem
kitesilk the mind at your ankles

Tides and grape-heaver grammar owl
more soft than agapanthi erotopythons

*

Her face could still last tone of swaying habit
as if by accident the sea
exactly.

*

Godparent beaker
thirst glued to drink
unbulimic fresh water

Spasm my brakes
downhill oaks
eros wind

Beacon praise
hourless night
poet-taken

*

Pansappho unscalp unfleece unscalpel
   unskin of flowers our kin

*

Lesmonia, Lemonanthis, Lesaromas, Lesvaia

*

Bird is drunk inside me
remembering the smell
at your door

You are the guest
heart traces

Out loud you fill
that doesn't exist

*

Justice missed hyperventilates poet
Buddha vowel in Mohammet child dared cross
far from mother olive groves father almonds
lyric sap of maple far from Lesvos

*

The soul has a knee
just risen just rinses

Laurel to air I speak your lips
lantern in the abyss

I am what astonishment can bear
tongue I owe you

Pupil only to you
fleece of dew

*

Owl to her narrow hipped tunic bread to her athlete sleep

small iconostasis clay girls
recombine danger and Homer

*

Dearest on the unrolled robe
young wife with peace in her hair

In the dark before the candle
where the archetypes take our unconscious to build
this work is forever

*

Wanderer gathers dusk in mountains
to its end the wind the stream
only riverbank hurry me

Only poetry

Gladys Cardiff

~ TO FRIGHTEN A STORM [1976]

Grey Woman

A woman coming down the snowy road
in moccasins, a basket on her arm,
her back bent by ninety Indian winters,
here to pick inside the garbage bins below
the porches on the Cheyenne reservation,
well-known among her people

Called Grey Woman. Finding a tin of sour
butter, she makes her way between the lines
of sheets that hang in rigid squares; each step
dependent on a frame less surely pinned
than frozen cloth cold-soldered to a wire.
She takes a rancid gob to eat.

Once the red Wyoming sun fell to her feet.
Young when the young men reeled, tied to the sun
and bringing it down, she watched one dance alone
on thongs sewn in his breast, his breath in blasts
that shook the twirling feathers on his pipe.
She hears the echo in her chirping heart,

The sound of day outlasted. The night she died,
following old belief, all doors were locked
until, after the manner of her ancestors,
she found *Maheo* and a final place.
The hand has turned to horn, and obdurate
Her spirit stands unhoused before my door.

Combing

Bending, I bow my head
and lay my hands upon
her hair, combing, and think
how women do this for
each other. My daughter's hair
curls against the comb,
wet and fragrant – orange
parings. Her face, downcast,
is quiet for one so young.

I take her place. Beneath
my mother's hands I feel
the braids drawn up tight
as piano wires and singing,
vinegar-rinsed. Sitting
before the oven I hear
the orange coils tick
the early hour before school.

She combed her grandmother
Mathilda's hair using
a comb made out of bone.
Mathilda rocked her oak wood
chair, her face downcast,
intent on tearing rags
in strips to braid a cotton
rug from bits of orange
and brown. A simple act
preparing hair. Something
women do for each other,
plaiting the generations.

Hayden Carruth

~ THE SLEEPING BEAUTY [1990]

15.

Called him "Big Joe" yes and Joe Turner it was his name
And he sang yes he sang
                                    well them deep down country blues
With a jump-steady and a K.C. beat   that came
From his big old heart and his bouncing shoes
From that big old bouncing voice

   Baby, you so beautiful and you gotta die someday

                              the same
As those Kansas City nights   huge boozy flame
Of the miserloos and the careless joys/   But slow
He could sing it too when it took him   sorrow
In the bone   slow

   Brokin the ten commanmint,
   Beat out with the jinx,
   Cain't sometimes
   Git water to drink,
   Ain't got a mount to jack in,
   Cain't produce a dime,
   I'm jus' as raggedy
   As a jay-bird in whistlin' ti
                         ime –

                              over and over
In the gathering of souls the flickering
Of human destiny that sways to discover
Happiness in fate.   And it was music, music.
"Shouter," they called him. And great is what he was,

Warm and   reckless   and accurate and   big –

Saint Harmonie,
    touch thou these lines with Turner's voice.

    112.

Your dream:
                The letters H I V appear
As if in blood on the wall of consciousness
And a voice comes out of the air,
Your own voice, saying, "Yes,
Human immunodeficiency virus, my dear,
For you in the heart of love."

                        So near,
The breakdown of nature? Was
Sexual order from which rose
Everything you know or make or see
So insubstantial, fallen
Like a house of cards now, jumbled, crazy
Useless? The wind still blows, the sullen
Sea still beats. You had only to think
A crack in reality, and there it is, appalling –
You and everyone standing there on the brink.

~ COLLECTED SHORTER POEMS [1992]

The Cows at Night

The moon was like a full cup tonight,
too heavy, and sank in the mist
soon after dark, leaving for light

faint stars and the silver leaves
of milkweed beside the road,
gleaming before my car.

Yet I like driving at night
in summer and in Vermont:
the brown road through the mist

of mountain-dark, among farms
so quiet, and the roadside willows
opening out where I saw

the cows. Always a shock
to remember them there, those
great breathings close in the dark.

I stopped, and took my flashlight
to the pasture fence. They turned
to me where they lay, sad

and beautiful faces in the dark,
and I counted them – forty
near and far in the pasture,

turning to me, sad and beautiful
like girls very long ago
who were innocent, and sad

because they were innocent,
and beautiful because they were
sad. I switched off my light.

But I did not want to go,
not yet, nor knew what to do
if I should stay, for how

in that great darkness could I explain
anything, anything at all.
I stood by the fence. And then

very gently it began to rain.

Sonnet

Well, she told me I had an aura. "What?" I said.
"An aura," she said. "I heered you," I said, "but
you ain't significating." "What I mean, you got
this fuzzy light like, all around your head,
same as Nell the epelectric when she's nigh read-
y to have a fit, only you ain't having no fit."
"Why, that's a fact," I said, "and I ain't about
to neither. I reckon it's more like that dead
rotten fir stump by the edge of the swamp on misty
nights long about cucumber-blossoming time
when the foxfire's flickering round." "I be goddamn
if that's it," she said. "Why, you ain't but sixty-
nine, you ain't a-rotting yet. What I say
is you got a goddamn naura." "OK," I said. "OK."

~ COLLECTED LONGER POEMS [1994]

from "Vermont"

Republicans? We've got a few. In fact
that's damned near *all* we had for a hundred years.
Then in '64 we went for Democrats,
the first time, went for the lesser evil
(that's what we thought) and gave our vote to Johnson
against Goldwater, and you can bet we won't
make that mistake again. Right now we have
a Democrat for governor, which isn't
a mistake exactly, it's an aberration.
I don't know if it's true, but I've been told
the poor guy suffers so much from loneliness
down there in Montpelier he has to call
a press conference just so he can find
someone to talk to. Mind, I don't say it's true.
Vermonters are Republican because
Bostonians are Democrats, that's all.
That's enough. Still there are Republicans

and Republicans. Take New Hampshire,
for instance; over there if you object
to the divine right of state senators
you're a Communist. Why hell, I knew a man
living in Coos Junction who wouldn't take
a twenty dollar bill; he couldn't stand
to carry Andrew Jackson in his pocket.
"Gimme two tens," he said. "Ain't it just like
them fathead red-tape artists? They design
the twenty for a red, then put a great man
like Hamilton on the tens." As far as I know
there's only one hereditary senator
in Vermont, and that's Fred Westphal from over
Elmore Mountain way. I don't know for sure
how Fred feels about Andy Jackson, but
he's carrying Elmore in his pocket and the rest
of his district too. Fred told a friend of mine
he'd never kissed a baby's face or a voter's
ass. I expect that's right. Of course it's not
exactly saying what he has done either
to keep himself down there in the legislature
since God knows when. "He's drawed his pay and 'tother
perquisites" – that's what my neighbor says.
My neighbor's an anarchist. That is to say,
a Vermonter, and that's to say, a Republican.
But just because he goes by the same label
as Nelson Rockefeller doesn't mean the two
have anything in common. They're worlds apart –
worlds. Ask my neighbor how he feels about
the government – the State with a capital S –
and what comes back is pure Bakuninism,
only of course with due allowances for different
times, places, idioms, and temperaments.
"Sons-of-bitches, every one of them" – that's
his feeling, and he means Rockefeller too,
or maybe especially. Why, I suspect
even Fred Westphal might be an anarchist,
though he'd turn the color of Ed Wipprecht's
best red cabbage if you accused him of it.
For my part, what's the use of stalling? I'm

an anarchist, have been for forty years,
only more a Warrenite than Bakuninite,
which is to say, nonviolent and independent,
or in other words American, which is what
lets me remain a patriot and a son
of the Founding Fathers, like my friend Paul Goodman –
Paul, the city Jew-boy who worked and fought
in New York all his life, fighting for virtue
or even for reason in an evil, crazy city,
and lost, and was always losing, which is why
he liked the country maybe and called his poems
hawkweeds and died three summers past – no, four –
over in Stratford underneath Percy Mountain.
The point is, there's a losing kind of man
who still will save this world if anybody
can save it, who believes . . . oh, many things,
that horses, say, are fundamentally preferable
to tractors, that small is more likable than big,
and that human beings work better and last longer
when they're free. Call him an anarchist,
call him what you will, a humanist,
an existentialist, hell, a Republican – names
are slippery, unreliable things. And yet
call him a Vermonter. That's what he is.

I don't say you can't find him in New Hampshire,
or even Maine – or Australia, for all I know –
the loser, the forlorn believer, the passer on.
But old Vermont is where I've found him mainly,
on the green mountain – on the western slope of it
if you want to be particular – where we talk
with that strange dialect which isn't exactly
Yankee, nor exactly anything else either.
"Calful" we say (as in *calf*), not "cahful,"
certainly not "careful," and what we make
our livings on, milking them morning and night,
are "kyeous." O.K. The further point is this:
we are still here, although we're passing on.

The Camps

FOR MARILYN HACKER

> *"Yes, art is palliative; but the substance of art is real.*
> *Can you make something from nothing?"*
>   *– Ivan Tolkachenko*

When the young brown-haired
woman was shot
a drop of blood swayed
briefly
on the end of her nose
and her baby brother for an instant
thought of a lantern.

> *

As the kittens were born
the father of the little girl
bashed the head
of each one against a rock.
She watched. This was
in another country. It was
in several other countries.

> *

The town is divided between those
who sit in a dark corner of what remains
of their houses
unwilling to see anyone

and those who go out into what remains
of the street
unwilling not to see everyone.

　　*

A sparrow flew into the high loft
above the people lying on the floor
and fluttered here and there crying
and cheeping as if trying to drink
the light at the crevices but at last
perched on a broken concrete strut
and closed its eyes.

　　*

The small pile of starved children
resembles the pile of brush
at the edge of a woods
in Alaska. Each will recede
into the earth at about
the same rate as the other.

　　*

Some always say the cats
or the crows or the ants
will be last,
but some insist
that the tough young women
and men will somehow endure,
will somehow prevail.

　　*

After they arrived
they spoke inventively in their language for a long time,
weeks and weeks,
contriving new snappy names for hunger,
for God and Satan,

for the machine,
until the subject itself faltered, and they were silent.

          *

For a second after the
sweep of bullets
he looked at himself cut in half.

          *

Who is it that stalks the camp?
Not the commandant, he has more sense.
Not the garbage-picker, there is no garbage.
Not that dying baobab tree over there.
Not the dew, there is no dew.
Not even the memory of the dew.
Yet we who are women bury our heads
in our hair and are still.
We who are children sprawl on the earth.
We who are men fold our hands and fall back
with our eyes wide.
Nobody knows who it is that stalks the camp.

          *

I am dying because I am black, one says.
Or because I am poor.
Or because I speak bad Spanish or Arabic.
Or because they found me in the Third Street Bar.
Or because my husband ran away.
You see, we are of the world in spite of everything
and we cling to the world's reasons.

          *

A little way apart from the long trudging
line of prisoners, a woman lay down
in the snow and gave birth. She was a sad

good-looking blonde. But I am not a woman,
she says. I cannot be, I refuse. Who is this dead
woman lying in the snow? No, I am a coyote.
And at once all the prisoners cried out softly
the coyote's song, which fills the gray air
from horizon to horizon and settles
upon the world. The newborn
coyote pup scampers away over the snow,
across the plain, into the forest.

*

Most of the starving children die peacefully
in their weakness, lying passive and still.
They themselves are as unaware of their
passing away as everyone else. But a few
haggard boys and girls at the last moment
twitch and open their eyes, and a sound
comes from their throats. Their eyes
express if only faintly knowledge
of their private dearness about to be
extinguished. They are struck by their superb
identities. Yes, these are the ones who . . . .

*

The world was never unbeautiful. All its parts,
marsh and savannah, forest and lake, scars
of lava and lightning and erosion, sparkled
in the sun. Now it has this camp and that one
and the thousands of others, camps almost
everywhere. Even the word *camp* once meant a field.

*

Sometimes children
become playthings.
A bit of their
intestines is pulled
out and handed

to them to see what
they will do with it.

        *

When an artillery shell falls
in a particular neighborhood, what follows
is an immediate exodus of body parts and other furniture,
and then the slower exodus. Usually
old people and children, but others too,
maimed and ill, mothers and cousins,
friends and strangers – an unlikely company – walking
in file, weak and unsteady, harried sometimes
by armed guards or sometimes not,
walking, walking, shuffling
through alleys, plazas, across bridges, out
along dusty roads, across the fields,
into the hills and forests.

        *

Following at a distance or waiting
in the shadows are wild dogs. Scream
if you can. Beg to be shot.

        *

And some are left behind, always in every village,
undiscovered, like this woman of forty
whose origin is doubtful. Is she black, white,
brown, yellow, pink? She is speckled.
Once she was plump and now her skin
sags around her like folds of dirty woolen
though she is nearly naked, and her wrinkled
dugs fall sideways where she is lying, her leg is
gangrenous, already part of the shinbone is showing
unexpectedly white. She is waiting for the sunrise
to bring her a little warmth while she
watches herself become a skeleton.

        *

He who is writing these words, an old man
on an undistinguished hillside
in North America
who has been writing for sixty years because this
is his way of being in the world, writing
on scraps of paper with stubby pencils
or on cheap tablets from the drug store, on a battered typewriter
set on an orange crate in a roach-ridden flat
in Chicago or in a small country house
on a computer, writing
all his life long
in the desert, on the mountain, in the forest,
on a beautiful boulder standing in the middle of a mountain brook,
writing,
writing year after year the way robins
build their nests . . .
What if these were his last words?
What if these sentences should be the vision at the end
of a lifetime he could never alter?

     *

Sing then of love
in the camps. Somebody
gives somebody else
a swallow of water.
People hold hands,
a woman cuddles her
baby as long as
she can. Men in the face
of the sweeping automatic
rifles against the wall
embrace just before
the blast. And does it
help? Ah how ardent
the hope has been! But
no one knows, the evidence
has vanished.

     *

In the simple tableau two brown women
lie with their hands
between each other's legs, worn-out
fingers resting in vulvas, a child
of eight or nine, turned aside, its sex
unknown, fondles itself but the arm fails
and drops down, a wife lies
with her husband's limp penis
against her cheek. Over the camp like descending
twilight the remnants of love
rest on the unmoving forms.

Testament

So often it has been displayed to us, the hourglass
with its grains of sand drifting down,
not as an object in our world
but as a sign, a symbol, our lives
drifting down grain by grain,
sifting away – I'm sure everyone must
see this emblem somewhere in the mind.
Yet not only our lives drift down. The stuff
of ego with which we began, the mass
in the upper chamber, filters away
as love accumulates below. Now
I am almost entirely love. I have been
to the banker, the broker, those strange
people, to talk about unit trusts,
annuities, CDS, IRAS, trying
to leave you whatever I can after
I die. I've made my will, written
you a long letter of instructions.
I think about this continually.
What will you do? How
will you live? You can't go back
to cocktail waitressing in the casino.
And your poetry? It will bring you

at best a pittance in our civilization,
a widow's mite, as mine has
for forty-five years. Which is why
I leave you so little. Brokers?
Unit trusts? I'm no financier doing
the world's great business. And the sands
in the upper glass grow few. Can I leave
you the vale of ten thousand trilliums
where we buried our good cat Pokey
across the lane to the quarry?
Maybe the tulips I planted under
the lilac tree? Or our red-bellied
woodpeckers who have given us so
much pleasure, and the rabbits
and the deer? And kisses? And
love-makings? All our embracings?
I know millions of these will be still
unspent when the last grain of sand
falls with its whisper, its inconsequence,
on the mountain of my love below.

Cyrus Cassells

Soul Make a Path Through Shouting

FOR ELIZABETH ECKFORD
LITTLE ROCK, ARKANSAS, 1957

Thick at the schoolgate are the ones
Rage has twisted
Into minotaurs, harpies
Relentlessly swift;
So you must walk past the pincers,
The swaying horns,
Sister, sister,
Straight through the gusts
Of fear and fury,
Straight through:
Where are you going?

I'm just going to school.

Here we go to meet
The hydra-headed day,
Here we go to meet
The maelstrom –

Can my voice be an angel-on-the-spot,
An amen corner?
Can my voice take you there,
Gallant girl with a notebook,
Up, up from the shadows of gallows trees
To the other shore:
A globe bathed in light,
A chalkboard blooming with equations –

I have never seen the likes of you,

Pioneer in dark glasses:
You won't show the mob your eyes,
But I know your gaze,
Steady-on-the-North-Star, burning –

With their jerry-rigged faith,
Their spear of the American flag,
How could they dare to believe
You're someone sacred?:
Nigger, burr-headed girl,
Where are you going?

I'm just going to school.

~ BEAUTIFUL SIGNOR [1997]

From the Theater of Wine

Gerona, Spain

Suddenly we're sons of Noah,
in Bible-beautiful robes,
wielding showy censers
to start with pomp
a Rosh Hashanah preschool pageant.
When the whirling incense
clears from the open courtyard
of the old kabbala school,
and the small children have quelled
their raucous coughing,
barrels of ripeness are brought in,
and tin pans
brimming with the vineyards' glory.
Soon Noah's mightily confused,
mock-intoxicated . . .

As you take a jesterly bow,
autumn sun glistens in the auburn

of your Old Testament wig.
And spry Noah is filling
the lush, tousled lap
of his lavish beard
with grapes.
And the barefoot children are learning
a fruit-breathed laughter
as they stamp and savor the labor
in the jubilant lesson of wine.

Paul Celan

~ EXILED IN THE WORD: POEMS & OTHER VISIONS OF THE JEWS
FROM TRIBAL TIMES TO THE PRESENT [1989]

A Death Fugue

Black milk of morning we drink you at dusktime
we drink you at noontime & dawntime we drink you at night
we drink & drink
we scoop out a grave in the sky where it's roomy to lie
There's a man in this house who cultivates snakes & who writes
who writes when it's nightfall *nach Deutschland* your golden hair Margareta
he writes it & walks from the house & the stars all start flashing he whistles
    his dogs to draw near
whistles his Jews to appear starts us scooping a grave out of sand
he commands us play up for the dance

Black milk of morning we drink you at night
we drink you at dawntime & noontime we drink you at dusktime
we drink & drink
There's a man in this house who cultivates snakes & who writes
who writes when it's nightfall *nach Deutschland* your golden hair Margareta
your ashen hair Shulamite we scoop out a grave in the sky where it's roomy to lie

He calls jab it deep in the soil you men you other men sing & play
he tugs at the sword in his belt & swings it his eyes are blue
jab your spades deeper you men you other men play up again for the dance

Black milk of morning we drink you at night
we drink you at noontime & dawntime we drink you at dusktime
we drink & drink
there's a man in this house your golden hair Margareta
your ashen hair Shulamite he cultivates snakes
He calls play that death thing more sweetly Death is a gang boss *aus Deutschland*
he calls scrape that fiddle more darkly then hover like smoke in the air
then scoop out a grave in the clouds where it's roomy to lie

Black milk of morning we drink you at night
we drink you at noontime Death is a gang-boss *aus Deutschland*
we drink you at dusktime & dawntime we drink & drink
Death is a gang-boss *aus Deutschland* his eye is blue
he hits you with leaden bullets his aim is true
there's a man in this house your golden hair Margareta
he sets his dogs on our trail he gives us a grave in the sky
he cultivates snakes & he dreams Death is a gang-boss *aus Deutschland*

your golden hair Margareta
your ashen hair Shulamite

Translated from the German by Jerome Rothenberg

Thomas Centolella

~ TERRA FIRMA [1990]

Small Acts

Whitman thought he could live with animals, they were
so placid and self-contained, not one of them dissatisfied.
I have lived with animals. They kept me up all night.
Not only tomcats on the prowl, and neurotic rats
behind my baseboards, scratching out a slim existence.
There were cattle next door in the butcher's pen,
great longhorns lowing in the dark. Their numbers had come up
and they knew it. I let their rough tongues lick my sorry palm.
Nothing else I could do for them, or they for me.

Walt can live with the animals. I'll take these vegetables on parade:
string beans and cabbage heads and pea brains, who negotiate
a busy crosswalk and feel brilliant, the smallest act accomplished
no mean feat, each one guiding them to other small acts
that will add up, in time, to something like steady purpose.
They cling to this fate, clutch it along with their brownbag lunches:
none of us would choose it, but this is their portion, this moment,
then this one, then the next. Little as it is, pitiful as it seems,
this is what they were given, and they don't want to lose it.

The gawky and the slow, the motley and the misshapen . . .
What bliss to be walking in their midst as if I were one of them,
just ride this gentle wave of idiocy, forget those who profess
an interest in my welfare, look passing strangers in the eye
for something we might have in common, and be unconcerned if nothing's there.
And now we peek into a dark café, and now we mug at the waitress
whose feet are sore, whose smiles makes up for the tacky carnations
and white uniform makes it easy to mistake her for a nurse,
even makes it necessary, given the state of the world.

And when the giant with three teeth harangues us to hurry up,
what comfort to know he's a friend, what pleasure to be agreeable,

small wonders of acquiescence, like obedient pets. Except animals
don't have our comic hope, witless as it is. They don't get
to wave madly at the waitress, as though conducting a symphony
of ecstatic expectations. If I turned and lived with animals
I'd only be a creature of habit, I'd go to where the food is
and the warmth. But I would get to say to my troubled friend,
"Your eyes are so beautiful. I could live in them."

~ LIGHTS AND MYSTERIES [1995]

The Woman of Three Minds

1.

She tells me she will find a letter
lying around the house – she lives
on the bay, she's intimate
with gray areas, with ebb and flow –
and she'll recognize the handwriting
as her own, but not what the sentences
mean to say. It's as if a cunning stranger
broke in when she wasn't home
and left these thoughts behind
for her benefit. Except, she says,
I have no idea what they mean.
And I'm afraid to read between the lines.

2.

And there's the local grocery store.
The old guy glued to his little TV
who winks at her when she comes in.
Last week, before she could open her mouth,
he tossed a pack of cigarettes on the counter.
"There you go," he said. It was some kind of joke
she didn't get. "I'm sorry," she said,
"but I don't smoke." "You mean you quit?"

"No, I mean I've never smoked."
The old guy laughed. "That's a good one.
You're always pulling my leg." And she saw
he was serious, this near stranger, laughing
at the antics of another near stranger.

3.

When she walked across the crowded yard
of the maximum security prison, the only woman
for miles, for years, an anesthetist on her way
to ease the stricken inmates into a useful sleep,
the healthy bold ones out for exercise
would edge close to the line they couldn't cross
without catching a bullet from the guards,
and they would take turns making sure she heard
all the usual four-letter words, plus their favorite
five-letter one, all the vilest fantasies
describing what goes where, and for how long,
and to what end – the manic vengeance of men
without hope, human souls who had begun their lives
exactly as she had.

4.

She told me she could handle any one of them.
Fear not a factor. None of them could come close,
she said, to what my father did to me.
Nonetheless, she couldn't wait to get one of them
on her table. A spinal tap would scare anyone
into humility, but when they found out who
was attending them, they'd freak. And what if
she let on she recognized them from the yard
and wasn't having a particularly good day?
And one day, as it happened, she got her wish:
the hard-time ringleader, fresh out of solitary,
a man for whom fear was not a factor either.

5.

His life was in her hands
but he worked his angles anyway. She couldn't know
who he was. He'd scam her with his best
model-inmate charm. Told her he'd known his share
of lookers, but she belonged in the movies,
not a hospital for degenerates. Even as she slipped
the needle in, he remained the smiling gentleman,
he made sure to hang on her every word,
never took his eyes off hers. She let him
play it out a while, it was the most amusement
she'd had in months. Then she interrupted him.
You know, she said, I know who you are.
It would be so easy to make sure
you never opened your mouth again.

6.

I walked down the dark pier once
where she lives alone in a simple house
that floats like a promise of safety
in a world of hidden dangers. All the lights out
except for one – the eerie purple neon
of an aquarium. If you stopped and looked hard,
you could see a night heron like the ghost of a bird
settled on a piling that was like death itself:
you couldn't see it, but you knew it had to be there.
And abandoned by the ramp to her front door:
the pale pink bicycle of a six-year-old.

7.

Do you know that poem, she asked me,
"I was of three minds, / Like a tree /
In which there are three blackbirds"?
It's something like that, except I never know
which mind will take over, or when.
But, I said, it's getting better for you, isn't it?

I guess so, she said… But I could see in her eyes
the small craft of the self slipping from its moorings,
pulled off to wherever the cold current would take it.
Yes, I'm better, she said, but with you I switch a lot:
I have no defense against kindness.

    8.

And I have no defense against helplessness,
the bête noire that springs up on a moment's notice:
a child, for instance, made to hide in the upstairs bathroom,
made to cower at the creak of someone mounting the stairs,
someone who had helped to create her world, and now,
night after night, is tearing it apart, limb by slender limb.
A child I can't save from the dreaded *snick snick*
of the door handle, which will turn too many times, even years later
in her own triple-locked house, as she sleeps in a loft bed, face down,
her hands folded over what she calls, for good reason, her privates.

    9.

After the hardtimer in the prison hospital
realized she valued respect over revenge,
he put out the word. The next day, as she crossed the yard,
one nightmare after another let her pass
without a sound. And then, at the end of the line,
a man with a scar from brow to jaw
bowed deeply and said, Good morning, ma'am,
and how are we today? And she said, We're just fine, thank you.
I looked at the woman of three minds and thought:
There are three important things in life. The first
is to be kind. The second is to be kind. And the third
is to be kind.

Joy

When it comes back to teach you
or you come back to learn
how half alive you've been,
how your ignorance and arrogance
have kept you deprived –
when it comes back to you
or you yourself return,
joy is simple, unassuming.
Red tulips on their green stems.
Early spring vegetables, bright in the pan.
The primary colors of a child's painting,
the first lessons, all over again.

Lucille Clifton

~ THE BOOK OF LIGHT [1993]

dear jesse helms

something is happening.
something obscene.

in the night sky
the stars are bursting

into flame. thousands
and thousand of lights

are pouring down onto
the children of allah,

and jesse,

the smart bombs do not recognize
the babies. something

is happening obscene.

they are shrouding words so that
families cannot find them.

civilian deaths have become
collateral damage, bullets

are anti-personnel. jesse,
the fear is anti-personnel.

jesse, the hate is anti personnel.
jesse, the war is anti-personnel,

and something awful is happening.
something obscene.

night vision

the girl fits her body in
to the space between the bed
and the wall. she is a stalk,
exhausted. she will do some
thing with this. she will
surround these bones with flesh.
she will cultivate night vision.
she will train her tongue
to lie still in her mouth and listen.
the girl slips into sleep.
her dream is red and raging.
she will remember
to build something human with it.

Cold Mountain

～ THE COLLECTED SONGS OF COLD MOUNTAIN [1983]

1.

storied cliffs were the fortune I cast
bird trails beyond human tracks
what surrounds my yard
white clouds nesting dark rocks
I've lived here quite a few years
and always seen the spring-water change
tell those people with tripods and bells
empty names are no damn good

71.

someone sits in a mountain gorge
cloud robe sunset tassels
handful of fragrances he'd share
the road is long and hard
regretful and doubtful
old and unaccomplished
the crowd calls him crippled
he stands alone steadfast

205.

my place is on Cold Mountain
perched on a cliff beyond the circuit of affliction
images leave no trace when they vanish
I roam the whole galaxy from here
lights and shadows flash across my mind
not one dharma comes before me
since I found the magic pearl
I can go anywhere everywhere it's perfect

Translated from the Chinese of Han Shan by Red Pine

Gerald Costanzo

⌒ BADLANDS [1973]

Everything You Own

Sometimes I think you're
from the South. You speak

with that drawl. You move
slowly as if taken by heat.

There are burning desires,
strange elevations you

never overcome. Everything
you own is in your

pockets. I see you in the
drugstore down on Main,

sipping soda, spitting
tobacco, mopping your brow.

You could tell me what this
country needs.

Sándor Csoóri

Somebody Consoles Me with a Poem

Can you hear it? Somebody's reading a poem to me over the telephone,
he's consoling me for my dead,
    for myself,
      he's promising a snowfall on my forehead,
snow on our common resting place:
    on a bed, forests, beyond the skeletons of yesterday's flowers,
and healing silence in a gentle cellar,
      where cut plum-tree logs
      will burn, blazing,
there will be wine on the table,
    onion
      and bread,
otherworldly light gleaming from a sharp knife,
and on the timeless, white cellar wall
    an ant, separated from its army,
      marches toward future centuries.
Can you hear it? What he says, he says to you as well:
    with big, black wings
      don't flap into the night,
        into mourning, into soot,
you're not an angel, nor a condor,
you're a sweet country's sole dweller,
    you're mine even though you're condemned to death!
      Your bound hair tumbles down
every night to my wrist
and I turn toward the North Star
    together with your back –
Weapons may stare at us tomorrow, too,
our misled country with thistly eyes,
we will no longer need your mercy:

we've lived everything that is life,
    everything that is the worry of people who die too early –
Look: the promised snow is falling softly already,
    down to our footprints advancing in pairs.

Translated from the Hungarian by Len Roberts and László Vértes

Michael Cuddihy

~ CELEBRATIONS [1980]

This Body

Each time breath draws through me,
I know it's older than I am.
The haggard pine that watches by the door
Was here even before my older brothers.
It's a feeling I get when I pick up a stone
And look at its mottled skin, the grey
Sleeve of time.
This body I use,
Rooted here, this hillside, leaves shaking in wind,
Was once as small as a stone
And lived inside a woman.
These words, even–
They've come such a long way to find me.
But the sleep that translates everything
Moves in place, unwearied, the whole weight of Ocean
That left us here, breathless.

Solitude

The large plate from the eighteenth century
When solitude was a Spanish word,
    soledad
Written across the center,
And the bird below, flying upside down, a ribbon
Like a worm around the neck, both ends
Dangling from his beak.

Without even a shrug of his wings
The bird has made

A fine hairline crack that fades out
Like an escape route.

Solitude – a worm that feeds on itself.
Each year its grip gets tighter.
And I, all night in my bed, flying,
The worm in my mouth,
Unable to swallow or spit it out.

Richard Dauenhauer

∼ IN THE DREAMLIGHT (TWENTY-ONE ALASKAN WRITERS) [1984]

Driving in a Snowstorm, King Salmon to Naknek

We leave the things of earth
behind: the river bottom, alder,
willow, birch and evergreen

for white becoming white,
the road defined by weeds
like runway lights

brown against the snow
on either side; the car
hurtles like a float plane

on a lake of snow, a taxi
on the step of tires, rushing
almost weightless, to the point

where the white strip curls
upward: lift off, where the road
parts from snowbound earth.

Madeline DeFrees

Beetle Light

FOR DANIEL HILLEN

Hornets collect on the side of the sun.
Windows I cannot open
magnify their frames. Whatever beam insinuates
itself in squares I cut across
fades the color underfoot and turns my aim
deadly. Sitting by your shade, dreaming
stained blue light, I weigh New England
dark against my palm and peer
through bottle green, milky accumulations
of the night.

       Overhead, black light in the socket,
broken neck of bulb, the filament
connected like a nerve. Someone has tried to get rid
of the irremovable shade, a welder's gun
turned against a coffee tin. Nailed to the rude
beam, nothing will bring it down. I return to antique
brass, your art and mine, to kerosene,
candlelight, flash of battery and morning rays,
small at first, burning away
the fog.

       Bodies accumulate. Small flies repelled
by cold. Dusky millers
stupefied in glare. You watched them cross your palm
and kept their silent iridescence
mounted in the brain, wings free as forms your glass
borrows. I prefer bugs at a distance: in plates,
in print, because I am less violent behind a screen.
Brittanica's hornet is sheer catharsis, a social

wasp, strikingly colored. The sting again.
Armed with a fly swatter, I watch one lift off the page,
begin to sing, the comb without the honey in the attic.
I darken towards the unexpected
spring. My plain-cooking landlady favors self-reliant
poets. They moon and thrive, trouble-free
tenants of the upper air. When I complain she mocks
the exterminator. Very soon they will die.

H.D.

⌒ PRIEST & A DEAD PRIESTESS SPEAKS [1983]

from "Priest"

VIII.

You come late;
you say,
"we are old;"

cold, cold, is the hand
that would draw you back,
cold, cold is death
but we are not old;

cold is life,
with a radium-heat more cold,
beautiful
(you are right)
and terrible,
(you are right)
life is more terrible than death,
but we are not old;

cold, cold is your breath,
cold is your face and your heart,
but not so cold
as the love that is radium,
that is my heart,
that has been my heart,
not so cold as the arrow, madness
that would slay
us
who forsakes life, desire,
not so cold as my love
that is burnished to withstand
even your fire.

Terry Ehret

Lost Body

after "Anatomy of Love"
by Ulalume Gonzales de Leon

One less
          possible day
opening and closing. There
we awaken, about to cross over
into the province of our beloved name.
As if the danger of brandishing this body
belonged to another. We do not know
where our blood is taken,
why our eyelids throb,
whether our hands can translate
what the heart repeats, its remote
cry.
     One less possible day repeating
with our arms, our skin, our knees
and the amorous nape of the neck
what it is like to be a body.
To lie in wait, opening and closing,
crossing from this body into the only other possible.
We utter our forgotten name to the one beloved,
as if to travel into that dangerous heart
were possible. As if it were possible
to be a body. As if we had never forgotten.

Odysseas Elytis

⌢ WHAT I LOVE [1986]

Sun the First

So often when I speak of the sun
In my tongue becomes tangled one
Large rose full of red.
But it is not bearable for me to be silent.

I.

I don't know anymore the night terrible anonymity of death
In the small turn of my soul a fleet of stars comes to port.
Guard of evening because you shine next to the sky-colored
Little wind of an island that dreams of me
Proclaiming the dawn from its tall boulders
My two eyes embrace and sail you with the star
Of my correct heart: I don't know anymore the night.

II. BODY OF SUMMER

Time has gone since the last rain was heard
Over the ants and lizards
Now sky burns without end
Fruit paint their mouth
Earth's pores open slowly slowly
And next to the water that drips syllabically
A huge plant looks the sun eye to eye!

Who is it lies on the high beaches
On his back toking silversmoked olive leaves
The cicadas are armed in his ears
Ants work in his chest
Lizards slide in the grass of underarm
And from his feet's kelp a wave lightly passing
Sent by the young siren who sang:

O body of summer nude burnt
Eaten by oil and by salt
Body of boulder and shiver of heart
Large windblown of the hair tree-graceful
Basilbreath over the curly pubes
Full of small stars and fir needles
Body deep sailship of the day!

Slow rains come rapid hailstorms
Land slinks by whipped in the nails of the snow
That bruises in the depths with savage waves
The hills plunge in the clouds' thick teats

And yet behind it all you smile without care
And find again your immortal hour
As the sun on the beaches finds you again
As in your naked health the sun

III.

Day shiny shell of the voice you made me by
Naked to walk in my daily Sundays
Among the welcome of the shores
Blow the first-known wind
Spread out the greens of tenderness
So that the sun may loll his head
And light the poppies with his lips
The poppies that the proud will scythe
To keep no sign on their naked chest
But the blood of defiance that undoes sorrow
Arriving at the memory of freedom

I spoke the love the health of the rose the ray
That alone directly finds the heart
Greece who with certainty steps on the sea
Greece who travels me always
On naked slow-glorious mountains.

I give my hand to justice
Transparent fountain source at the peak
My sky is deep and unaltered

What I love is always being born
What I love is beginning always.

   IV.

Drinking Corinthian sun
Reading the marbles
Climbing over arbor seas
Targeting with the fishing spear
A covenant fish that slips
I found the leaves the sun's psalm has by heart
The live dry land desire rejoices
To open.

I drink water I cut fruit
I shove my hand in the leafy wind
The lemon trees irrigate the pollen of summer
Green birds tear my dreams
I leave in a glance
Eyes wide where the world becomes again
Beautiful from the beginning to the measurement of the heart.

Translated from the Greek by Olga Broumas

~ THE LITTLE MARINER [1988]

from "Anoint the Ariston"

   X.

Whatever I was able to acquire in my life by way of acts visible to all, that is, to
   win my own transparency, I owe to a kind of special courage Poetry gave me:
   to be wind for the kite and kite for the wind, even when the sky is missing.

I'm not playing with words. I mean the movement you discover being written in
   an "instant," when you can open it and make it last. When, in fact, Sorrow be-
   comes Grace and Grace Angel; Joy Alone and Sister Joy

with white, long pleats over the void,

a void full of bird dew, basil breeze and a hiss of resonant Paradise.

Translated from the Greek by Olga Broumas

⁓ SELECTED & LAST POEMS [1997]

from "With Light & With Death"

18.

Even when they destroy you it will still be beautiful
The world because of you
              your heart – true heart
In place of what they took from us –
Will still beat and a gratitude
From the trees you touched will cover us

Unshackled lightning how do they retie you

Now that I have no air no animal companion
Nor even a woodsman's lost thunderbolt
I hear water running
           maybe from God
(And I blaspheming) or from the mouth
Of a solitary who approached the peak's most Secret Keys
And opened them
              for this I address You
Night of a Holy Tuesday with the irreplaceable pelago
Facing me – so you can tell it goodbye and thanks.

Translated from the Greek by Olga Broumas

from "Anoint the Ariston"

XXVII.

I was late in understanding the meaning of humility, and it's the fault of those
who taught me to place it at the other end of pride. You must domesticate the
idea of existence in you to understand it.

One day when I was feeling abandoned by everything and a great sorrow fell
slowly on my soul, walking across fields without salvation, I pulled a branch
of some unknown bush. I broke it and brought it to my upper lip. I under-
stood immediately that man is innocent. I read it in that truth-acerbic scent so
vividly, I took its road with light step and a missionary heart. Until my deep-
est conscience was that all religions lie.

Yes, Paradise wasn't nostalgia. Nor, much less, a reward. It was a right.

Translated from the Greek by Olga Broumas

As Endymion

Exactly like the upper life sleep has
Its tender valleys. With little churches grazing
                    grass before the air
Chewing until they turn to icons
Erasing each other in a sideways sound. Often
Two or three moons promenade. But soon they fade
Beauty endures the pause as a celestial body
Matter has no age. Change is all it knows.
Take it from the start or end. Return flows calmly
Forward and you follow
Feigning indifference but pulling
The rope to a deserted Myrtle cove
Not missing an olive tree
Oh sea
You wake and everything renews!
We were so dandled tossing our genes for jacks!
See what a rise Sirocco Sleep gets from the placid
                    dividing it in two! On one
Side I wake and weep for my delights were taken
And on the other sleep
While Eleutherios leaves and Ionia fades
A low hill barely visible
Its tender bellies full of curly greens
Opposite it harsh contestments
How guard against contingency
When refugee bees swarm and a grandmother
Among misfortune's fisheries succeeds
To eke from her few gold ornaments kids and grandkids

Get rid of danger and it rolls you down one side ignores you
As you had wanted to ignore it once
Undo it all now in the sham of your unlined garment
Where soot and gold coins touched
Like slime on the holy
                    Strange

How blindly we live yet hang by it
Fresh dove of basil kiss I gave you on my bed
And in my writings three and four unorthographic winds
To dazzle the pelagi but full
Of mind and knowledge keep each vessel on its course
Events do lurch and in the end
Fall down before the humans
But dark has no lantern in the storm
Where's Miletos where Pergamos
                        Attaleia and where
Constant   tino   tinopolis?
In a thousand sleeps one comes awake
                        but it's forever

Artemis Artemis grab me the moon's dog
It bites a cypress and unsettles the Eternals
Much deeper sleeps whom History has drenched
Strike it a match like alcohol
                        it's only Poetry
Remains. Poetry. Just and essential and direct
As Adam and Eve imagined it. Just
In the pungent garden and infallible to clocks.

Translated from the Greek by Olga Broumas

Carolyn Forché

Ourselves or Nothing

for Terence Des Pres

After seven years and as the wine
leaves and black trunks of maples wait
beyond the window, I think of you
north, in the few lighted rooms
of that ruined house, a candle in each
open pane of breath, the absence of anyone,
snow in a hurry to earth, my fingernails
pressing half moons into the sill
as I watched you pouring three
then four fingers of Scotch over ice,
the chill in your throat like a small
blue bone, those years of your work
on the Holocaust. You had to walk
off the darkness, miles of winter
riverfront, windows the eyes in skulls
along the river, gratings in the streets
over jeweled human sewage, your breath
hanging about your face like tobacco.
I was with you even then, your face
the face of a clock as you swept
through the memoirs of men and women
who would not give up. In the short light
of Decembers, you took suppers of whole
white hens and pans of broth
in a city of liquor bottles and light.
Go after that which is lost
and all the mass graves of the century's dead
will open into your early waking hours:
Belsen, Dachau, Saigon, Phnom Penh
and the one meaning Bridge of Ravens,
São Paulo, Armagh, Calcutta, Salvador,

although these are not the same.
You wrote too of Theresienstadt,
that word that ran screaming into
my girlhood, lifting its grey wool dress,
the smoke in its violent plumes and feathers,
the dark wormy heart of the human desire to die.
In Prague, Anna told me, there was bread,
stubborn potatoes and fish, armies and the women
who lie down with them, eggs perhaps but never
meat, never meat but the dead.
In Theresienstadt she said there was only the dying.
Never bread, potatoes, fish or women.
They were all as yet girls then.
Vast numbers of men and women died, you wrote,
*because they did not have time, the blessing
of sheer time, to recover.* Your ration of time
was smaller then, a tin spoon of winter,
piano notes one at a time from the roof
to the gutter. I am only imagining this,
as I had not yet entered your life
like the dark fact of a gun on your pillow,
or Anna Akhmatova's "Requiem"
and its final *I can* when the faceless woman
before her asked *can you describe this?*
I was not yet in your life when you turned
the bullet toward the empty hole in yourself
and whispered: finish this or die.
But you lived and what you wrote became
The Survivor, that act of contrition for despair:
*They turned to face the worst
straight-on, without sentiment or hope,
simply to keep watch over life.* Now,
as you sleep face down on your papers,
the book pages turning of themselves
in your invisible breath, I climb
the stairs of that house, fragile
with age and the dry fear of burning
and I touch the needle to music to wake you,
the snow long past falling, something
by Vivaldi or Brahms.
I have come from our cacophonous

ordinary lives where I stood at the sink
last summer scrubbing mud from potatoes
and listening to the supper fish
in the skillet, my eyes on the narrowed
streets of rain through the window
as I thought of the long war
that misted country turned to the moon's surface,
grey and ring-wormed with ridges of light.
the women in their silk *ao dais* along
the river, those flowers under fire, rolled
at night in the desperate arms of American men.
Once I walked your rooms with my
nightdress open, a cigarette from my lips
to the darkness and back as you worked
at times through to the morning.
Always on my waking you were gone,
the blue holes of your path through snow
to the road, your face still haggard
in the white mirror, the pained note
where ten times you had written
the word *recalcitrance* and once:
you will die and live under the name of someone
who has actually died.
I think of that night in a tropic hotel,
the man who danced with a tray over his head
and offered us free because we were *socialistas*,
not only that, he sang, but young and pretty.
Later as I lay on a cot in the heat naked
my friend was able to reach for the guns
and load them clicking in the moonlight
with only the barest of sounds;
he had heard them before me moving among the palms.
We were going to die there.
I remember the moon notching its way
through the palms and the calm sense that came
for me at the end of my life. In that moment
the woman beside me became my sister,
her hand cupping her mouth, the blood
that would later spill from her face
if what we believed was the truth.
Her blood would crawl black and belly-down

onto a balcony of hands and flashlights,
cameras, flowers, propaganda.
Her name was René and without knowing
her you wrote: *all things human take time,*
time which the damned never have, time for life
to repair at least the worst of the wounds;
it took time to wake, time for horror
to incite revolt, time for the recovery
of lucidity and will.
In the late afternoons you returned,
the long teeth shining from the caves,
a clink in the wood half-burnt
and as you touched it alive:
ici repose un déporté inconnu.
In the mass graves, a woman's hand
caged in the ribs of her child,
a single stone in Spain beneath the olives,
in Germany the silent windy fields,
in the Soviet Union where the snow
is scarred with wire, in Salvador
where the blood will never soak
into the ground, everywhere and always
go after that which is lost.
There is a cyclone fence between
ourselves and the slaughter and behind it
we hover in a calm protected world like
netted fish, exactly like netted fish.
It is either the beginning or the end
of the world, and the choice is ourselves
or nothing.

James Galvin

~ ELEMENTS [1988]

Post-Modernism

A pinup of Rita Hayworth was taped
To the bomb that fell on Hiroshima.
The Avant-garde makes me weep with boredom.
Hares *are* wishes, especially dark ones.

That's why twitches and fences.
That's why switches and spurs.
That's why the idiom of betrayal.
They forgive us.

Their windswayed manes and tails,
Their eyes,
Affront the winterscrubbed prairie
With gentleness.

They live in both worlds and forgive us.
I'll give you a hint: the wind in fits and starts.
Like schoolchildren when the teacher walks in,
The aspens jostle for their places

And fall still.
A delirium of ridges breaks in a blue streak:
A confusion of means
Saved from annihilation

By catastrophe.
A horse gallops up to the gate and stops.
The rider dismounts.
Do I know him?

Two Horses and a Dog

Without external reference,
The world presents itself
In perfect clarity.

Wherewithal, arrested moments,
The throes of demystification,
Morality as nothing more
Than humility and honesty, a salty measure.

Then it was a cold snap,
Weather turned lethal so it was easier
To feel affinity
With lodgepole stands, rifted aspens,
And grim, tenacious sage.

History accelerates till it misses the turns.
Wars are shorter now
Just to fit into it.

One day you know you are no longer young
Because you've stopped loving your own desperation.
You change *life* to *loneliness* in your mind
And, you know, you need to change it back.

Statistics show that
One in every five
Women
Is essential to my survival.
My daughter asks how wide is lightning.
That depends, but I don't know on what.
Probably the dimension of inner hugeness,
As in a speck of dirt.

It was an honor to suffer humiliation and refusal.
Shame was an honor.

It was an honor to freeze your ass horseback
In the year's first blizzard,
Looking for strays that never materialized.

It was an honor to break apart against this,
An honor to fail at well-being
As the high peaks accepted the first snow –
A sigh of relief.
Time stands still
And we and things go whizzing past it,
Queasy and lonely,
Wearing dogtags with scripture on them.

⌣ RESURRECTION UPDATE: COLLECTED POEMS [1997]

Station (1)

Its back was leaves that mimed the leaves in back of us, but
the chair was painted white – white as the snow that never
stopped falling in my ears.
                          The white leaves of the chair
that mocked the leaves of the back-drop, making us, for you,
the fore-drop, imprinted leaf-prints on my bare back – white
ones.
       I held my gurgling sister in my lap, child whose cloud
I held as well, as the white wrought chair with its white leaves
sped us toward the sanctuary of damage.
                                    Can you, where you are
now, remember the garden chair I held her in for you?
                                              We make
a crazy Pietà, my newborn sister and I.
                                 You step back.
                                          In my
lap there rests a cloud of swaddling blankets like a shroud,
and on the cloud a laughing child.
                              I squint and smile.
                                           I'm round-
faced as a moon on a string, tow-headed, slope-shouldered, vague

as a lamb and shorn like one.
                              The backdrop won't drop back
its ivied wall.
                    I'm six and looking at you as if to have my
picture snapped.

Station (2)

I was teaching my little sister how to fly when she broke her
arm.
        I did.
                    I lay back in the snow and put my galoshes against
her skinny butt and pushed her into the sky.
                                        Over and over up-
ward into the falling, and the fallen caught her, and her laughter
spilled.
            We got it wrong one time and that was it.
                                        I said, "Now,
now."
        My mother's white station wagon disappeared into the snow
on its way to the white hospital, and the volume turned up.

Right now a spring snow falls and sublimes.
                                        The snowline retreats
upward like a rising hem of sky.
                        The snow is disappearing toward
me.

Station (4)

Somewhere between a bird's nest and a solar system whom did
the story use to fashion the crown of thorns, and did it prick
them?
            Whom did the story use for judgement?
                                        Whom for betrayal?

The slender silver filament of drool from too much Quaalude
tethered her chin to her shoulder.
                                        When I came back she was
sitting on the couch, her hands turned up, her face turned
away and down.
                        Every Annunciation is freaked with doom, flashed
in crucifixion.
                        Because I left home she was allowed to keep
pushing her face through windshields of collapsing cars,
as if she wanted to be born from a speeding automobile.
                                                        All
according to plan, following the story in telling it.
                                        Pilate
no more judges Christ than he judges the air he breathes.
                                                        He
is nothing.
                        He washes his hands according to plan, another
symbol.
                It would be like judging cloud formations, the Grand
Canyon, or an ant.
                        Like washing less than nothing from your
hands.

Ken Gerner

Prey

Early light on the meadow
moves through dew
to touch your eyes

with shadows of fading stars.
Down in damp grass,
we lie warm.

Stones urge us out of bed,
matted grass rises after us,
low limbs burst with fire.

With a cry, the hawk begins
his spin. Brown feathers
weave into blue. The sun,
the tea, steam.

Your hand lies
soft, small, in mine.
A mouse stirs
in the morning grass.

House of Breath

Over the Coast Range, silver horns of cloud
darken to rose. The fire is set. The crackle
and pop of pitch and kindling burn into logs.
I split ribs for dinner, aware of thin muscles
that hold the dark cave of breath. This house

welcomes as winter approaches. There were others.
One of logs in a valley in the Rockies, where
I was raised roughhousing with my father
and brothers. The years winter ran late,
my father's hands cracked from the waters
of calving and wind. Later, that wind
out of the Gulf of Alaska bowed the tops

of second-growth on the peninsula's tip. Inside,
warm, I watched chunks of turnips and spuds
fall into the pot of stew as I talked with
friends in their house of poetry and printing,
of what it is to love something, anything.
Bourbon has never been so smooth. Searing ribs.

Soon my love will return to enter this warmth,
the cascade of smells and she will smile at the half-
empty bottle. I will sit as this house asks her
what she remembers, watch as her children dance
across her eyes. The warmth of other fires
will become her arms curled under her breasts,
around the rise and fall of her breathing.

And then one of us will say something silly,
like "how's your ass" and laugh at the infinity
of intention and the simple charms we use
to enter the silence. Outside, the wind
will come with its dreams of snow. We will
be shadows crossing shafts of yellow light.

Fat from the ribs will shine our cheeks as
we eat by the fire and coals will glow
as we make love beside bowls of bones and
light echoing in glasses empty of wine.

In the morning, I will leave the warmth of bed.
There will be frost and the cold floor.
The rags of alder leaves droop as I step outside
to sit with the morning, to watch smoke drift
from houses in this hollow. Cold and empty,
my lungs will fill and my ribs shudder around
and hold to the fine precision of breath.

Patricia Goedicke

Imprint of Microscopic Life Found in Arctic Stones

Blood splatters itself on snow:
Scarlet pomegranate seeds wink.

Out there in the white swamps, in barren fields of eyes

Hunger rackets through the air. Battered Chinese
Bleak pagodas, long blue centipedes.

Armies of anonymity advance,

But still there are flowers growing: magenta shreds on the peachstone,
Pink turnips in the root cellar.

Louder than jets I sing

For every miniature fossil locked
Motionless, in the old bones

But not vanquished, never:

With the small blood booming in our ears
It is always time to stand up,

In the farthest forests listen:

Bushes scratch at the stars, even the mole
Has velvet skin, and never goes too far.

Deceived by twitches and greed

Where there are too many leaders too many will be trampled
But either extreme is wrong, we are not helpless,

Neither have we any power but what we are given is ours

In fierce showers from the sun, in the vicious blast of a windstorm
Each particle rises, hordes upon hordes suspended

In the fine sting of blizzards forty degrees below zero

At the North Pole as at the South Pole each atom is alive
And fighting for it:

Though we are not heroes we contain all

Memory and the frozen memory of memory:
Neither are we stones but there are microscopic codes

In icy rock hidden, at each end of the world
In a dream of mastodons beyond all measurement breathing.

Susan Griffin

~ UNREMEMBERED COUNTRY [1987]

Ordinary, as Love

Love between women,
you don't know this yet!
How can I put it into words?
Think of the face of that singer,
the way her hand went to her temple.
Imagine yourself, you listen
as she sings the highest note.
You have taken in the air of silence
and while this silence leaves your body
you are becoming sound. Now
you are so close to that singer
you rise and fall with her breath.
But this may be too strong.
Think then of a warm wind
so gentle, so subtle you can
scarcely see it as it
holds you, not touching but
hovering so near, so
near you feel the field of gravity
and in the grip of this breeze
you who are transfixed like stone
have become light too, part air
part color, brushed
by the softest wings
while you taste this
insubstantial substance
that dissolves inside you. But
perhaps this is too pale.
Think then of a longing.
You are afraid to want so much.
Those wings that brushed you
recede into night, this night with

eyes so black they are endless
and you have fallen
fallen as far as you can measure
and are still falling
God help you
pray as you
descend, remember
you are only human
the sun will rise
there will be a day again, though
you don't know this yet,
a day, ordinary as love, a day
familiar as women.

⌣ COLLECTED POEMS [1997]

To the Far Corners of Fractured Worlds

I.

How would you
catch it
your hand on a pencil
tracing the
outlines?
A leg
entangled
with another leg
or heavy there
and hands
six or eight grasping,
holding like clamps

II.

And there would be some
fabric, pieces of a skirt

frayed rope, soiled, used and reused for
different purposes
hauling water, keeping the trunk of a
car closed and
this.

And there might also be
pieces of metal
making a chain
that encircles
goes around the body
around and around

III.

Then, of course
you lose it
your painterly command
you cannot draw
you cannot imagine how
you want to bring in
one of the old masters
one with the largest possible canvas
the one who painted creation on the ceiling
of consciousness
to paint this
because the gaping space
your hands feel in the thick of
your inaction
is that wide.

IV.

Or perhaps
the portrait could show
a quiet moment
one that preceded
what is happening,
peaceful in a
misleading sort of

way
like that portrait
from the seventeenth century showing
successful burghers
all in a row
all well-dressed
some fully illuminated
standing forward, proud
others barely visible
a shadow crossing those faces.
And behind,
a deeper darkness.

v.

But what you witness now
is not still
and your own eyes are
moving, moving
darting, looking up, away, shutting,
madly skipping
in the craziest dance,
dancing with what they see
all the way to the edge of
motion.

vi.

And what is this dance
our eyes follow?

The music
so strange
that high thin song
with the odd blue sound
and the cracking.

Is that how they sound
old bones?

VII.

Of course, gentlemen,
we hear you too
as you explain,
she is not your
Grandmother

and this is not
your child either,
you tell us,
whose throat
just closed.

VIII.

And who are you?
You are of course only human.
The curled paper
on which light has burned
the image of those you love
has grown damp with
heat
in your pocket.
You are tired.
Understandably so.
The tears you shed
twenty deaths back
are packed like ice
against the sore
stiffness that has
invaded you.
Just this morning
you woke alert
frightened at the soundlessness
of death, until
the smell of coffee
burned on the fire
reached you.
Then, brushing the sleep from

your eyes,
you spent long moments carefully polishing
patiently threading the
necessary pieces of metal together
placing the eyepiece in line
with the proper instrument
so that all life
as you once knew it lay
composed
before that delicate juncture where
two stitch-thin cross hairs
meet.

    IX.

Try to compose it,
it fails
the center
vanishes

the figures
suddenly
nowhere
in sight

or hiding under
scraps of buildings
the columns of a fallen bridge
any thing hard will do
as shield
or carapace

yet nothing stays
everything disperses
you cannot draw this
dust as it rises

and when
as the air clears
you are met

by the shock of a
body newly rent

your hands fly
off the page.

    x.

But of course
you can work from memory.
Were you the child who watched
as her sister was dragged beneath the house
by that gaggle of boys?
Were you followed
on the way home
yourself and pulled
flat? And if you escaped
still, so often and
quickly, quickly
you look back.

    xi.

It is not so much a canvas that is needed
as an ocean
or a sky.
And you cannot paint this alone.
You could drown in this picture.
There are waves here
which sink
the safest ships and you must
break
to hear them.

    xii.

Consider then
the many perspectives
that are needed
or are

silent partners in this
arrangement, the viewpoint
of the lens at different ranges
upward to cosmic bodies perhaps exercising
their pull, inward to the cell, whose boundaries
are so transparent, down into the world of the
dead from whom all else is built,
or the viewpoint of the ones who make the lens,
who adjust the aperture
who make the metal casing,
ring after ring
which houses vision,
or those who make the other objects
bracelets, fences,
the moving parts of machines. Or
the viewpoint of those spinning
the thinnest threads
who weave our names into a cloth
that is laid upon the table
and the ones who sow
and collect what is there later
in the fields
and those who make bread
this vision is also needed.

XIII.

And there is another angle of sight
wholly impossible
what is unwitnessed
and must remain so
because all that we know
approaches
but does not enter.

Only those who have entered know
those who have been forced
to a knowledge that has
severed knowing
into the smallest pieces

fragments flying into
the far corners of a fractured world.

XIV.

So it remains to reassemble
whatever we can
on this holy or unholy day
on this day like any other
remembering
letting words fall into our mouths
like bits of a
shared meal
scanning the numerous texts,
rendering all the possible
readings,
scriptures various as
seeds, the many meanings
of this feast
the spilled wine of
our living.

XV.

And if given
what we see
every move
is riddled with pause
here in the hesitation
is where
the hand searching the page
first touches form.

Though so much is missing
still it is here
you can begin to imagine
the arc of vision
bending home.

And though the severed
still shiver
inside
this circle
here is a place
we can meet

one to the other
the other to one.

John Haines

⌐ IN THE DREAMLIGHT (TWENTY-ONE ALASKAN WRITERS) [1984]

If the Owl Calls Again

at dusk
from the island in the river,
and it's not too cold,

I'll wait for the moon
to rise,
then take wing and glide
to meet him.

We will not speak,
but hooded against the frost
soar above
the alder flats, searching
with tawny eyes.

And then we'll sit
in the shadowy spruce and
pick the bones
of careless mice,

while the long moon drifts
toward Asia
and the river mutters
in its icy bed.

And when morning climbs
the limbs
we'll part without a sound,

fulfilled, floating
homeward as the
cold world awakens.

Nocturnal

Missing the noise of the sea at night,
I find it difficult to sleep.
    Difficult to be content with the tame
sounds of human habitation:
somebody's dog barking, somebody's
door swinging to,
a window raised in a nearby house,
the hum and crunch of a passing car...
    And not long for the primitive rhythm
of the tides, the peep of peewits,
and the sound of the wind in the grass.

Provincetown, 1951

Evening Change

Beautiful light down there
where the dark hills open
    toward the sea,
and the promontory groves
show like the ruined towers
of castles older than thought –
    Even this sordid valley
seems sweet and hallowed now,
where birds cross in the twilight,
unwatched by jealous eyes.

Carmel Valley, 1952

Mark Halperin

⌒ A PLACE MADE FAST [1982]

Two Lines from Paul Celan

At nightfall the sky was various
blues and grays moving into each other.
You drew the drapes then gathered
with the others before the wireless,
only you listening to the leaves
fill like teacups. Then the war was over

and you lived in this foreign city
where you have slipped on a raincoat
and gone for the evening paper.
Behind a warehouse, the yellow moon
rises, bearing your lost mittens
and the copybook between whose ruled veins

you had seen the sky at Gilgal
keeping light wonderfully, a drama
of finite scope, finite duration.
The next day, your parents packed
an overnight bag. Smoke
widens at the tall brick stacks

east of you. They never returned.
The boy who dashes past bends
his head, but you have seen his eyes,
blue or brown as your own. You lift
your collar and cross one of the bridges,
pass beneath the streetlamps, from light

to dark, from dark to light,
to your own door. You've forgotten
the paper, but the mittens are
recollected and, safely, the copybook too.

At your back, leaves turn over. The wind
spills them carrying a Russian song.

The sun stood still; the moon halted.
A circus? the seacoast? Out of what
other contradiction could you hope
to render such implacable grief:
things lost were not lost,
the heart was a place made fast.

Sam Hamill

〜 ANIMAE [1980]

Reading Seferis

TO OLGA BROUMAS

"Not many moonlit nights
have given me pleasure."
The stars spell out
the ancient mathematics
of the heart in huge
desolate zeros, ciphers
of nothing, and despite it all,
I care. There is a fatigue
in the crumbling of cities
for which there is no cure,
no penance or catharsis,
not even a prayer – only
the will to endure. The heavy
torpor of gray-brown air,
the lethargy of the soul –
by these we measure out
each crisis, each ancient debt
we don't repay the poor.

There are not many moons
I remember. The Sound
is blue where it reflects
the dark sky of night
or the bright sky of day.
Amica silentia lunae,
and each day the sun
drowns in fire and water,
a metaphor for nothing,
our unaccountable longing.
Some would call upon the moon
for power, for pure sexual

pleasure, but that is unholy
and denies both the sowing
and the reaping. The moon
is not a scythe that mows
the tall mute grass of heaven.

But we, Olga, are grasses
wavering in breezes
of politics and dollars, we
are the exiles of the earth,
the rooted and swarthy who see
the moon in everything
and think it a symbol
for our suffering. It is
the human mind that curves
into a razor, that harvests
human pain. We shall be
the chaff which flies
in the cutting, the lullaby
of fields that is not heard
on moonless nights because
only moonlight is romantic.

I hear the lullaby of victims
who are happy. Few are the moons
for them, and even these
are imagined. I imagine the
full moon of a smile, the moon
of my buttocks when I was a boy
and a prankster, the twin
moons of my lover's breasts,
the stars, oh, in her eyes
and I love her. Olga, these
are the maps, topographies
of the heart that tell us
everything: we are all
the victims; we are heroes
also, and slaves. Seferis says
heroes are the ones
move forward in the dark.

I remember the terrible
darkness of my childhood
and the fear. And the moon
was more fearsome, more awe-full
with its wails and howls
and its shadows. I remember
the moon as female, Loba, yesterday
when she raged. I tire so soon
of metaphor! I want to send you,
Olga, this alphabet of stars
which ask for nothing
and offer a little light
against the dark we wear;
I want to offer the warmth
of a lullaby, the kiss
of deep sleep, a reflection of the moon
reflected on the waters
of your song – so few

are the moonlit nights
that I've cared for.

~ DESTINATION ZERO (WHITE PINE PRESS) [1995]

The Gift of Tongues

Everything I steal, I give away.
Once, in pines almost as tall as these,
same crescent moon sliding gently by,
I sat curled on my knees, smoking with a friend,
sipping tea, swapping coyote tales and lies.

He said something to me
about words, that each is a name,
and that every name is God's. I who have
no god sat in the vast emptiness silent
as I could be. *A way that can be named*

is not the way. Each word reflects
the Spirit which can't be named. Each word
a gift, its value in exact proportion
to the spirit in which it is given.
Thus spoken, these words I give

by way of Lao Tzu's old Chinese, stolen
by a humble thief twenty-five centuries later.
The Word is only evidence of the real:
in the Hopi tongue, there is no whale;
and, in American English, no Fourth World.

Han Yü

Poem on Losing One's Teeth

Last year I lost an
incisor and this year a molar
and now half a dozen
more drop out at once –
and that's not the end of it
either. The rest are all loose
and there won't be an end
till they're gone.

The first one
I thought what a shame, what
an obscene gap! Two or three –
I was falling apart – almost
you might say, at death's door.

Before
when one loosened I'd quake
and hope wildly it "wouldn't."
The gaps made it hard to
chew and a loose tooth I'd
rinse my mouth gingerly.
Then when at last
it would fall out it felt
like a mountain collapsing.
By now I've got used to it
nothing earthshaking.

I've still twenty
left though I know one by one
they'll all go.
But at one tooth per year
it will take them two decades

and gone will it matter
they went one by one and not
as a single disaster?

Folks say
when your teeth go, the end's
near. But I think
all life has its limits –
when you die you die
whether with or without teeth.
They also say gaps
scare the people who see you.
Well, two views to everything
as Chuang-tzu noted.

A blasted
tree need not always be cut down
though geese that don't hiss
be slaughtered. For the toothless
who mumble, silence
can be an advantage and those
who can't chew may discover
that soft food is tastier.

This is a poem I chanted
and wrote down to startle my
wife and children.

Translated from the Chinese by Kenneth O. Hanson

Paul Hansen

⌒ BEFORE TEN THOUSAND PEAKS [1980]

Moored for the Night at the Lan-chi Riverside Courier Station

I close my eyes; waves blow against the pillow.
Open the awning, the moon comes in the boat.
How strange! Riverwater draws the sky
The second watch of night.

My remaining want: Get high on pure enjoyment,
Overturn sadness and defeat the drunken daze.
Tonight I cling to twilight yesterday.
It is raining; I lie down
Before ten-thousand peaks.

From the Chinese of Yang Wan-li

Gerald Hausman

Appaloosa Hail Storm

Hauled hay bales all afternoon
saddle blankets, wet with sweat
dry on a fence in the sun.

Stalls full, one wheelbarrow load
of hot sweet manure
tips on thin plank out back.

Suddenly the sky is all summer storm.
I sit on my overturned wheelbarrow
and watch an appaloosa explode into hail.

Robert Hedin

~ SNOW COUNTRY [1975]

Transcanadian

At this speed, my friend, our origins are groundless.
We are nearing the eve of a great festival,
The festival of wind.
Already you can see this road weakening.
Soon it will breathe
And lift away to dry its feathers in the air.
On both sides the fields of rapeseed and sunflowers
Are revolting against their rows.
Soon they will scatter wildly like pheasants.
Now is the time, my friend, to test our souls.
We must let them forage for themselves,
But first – unbuckle your skin.
Out here, in the darkness
Between two shimmering cities,
That we have, perhaps for the last time, chance
Neither to be shut nor open, but to let
Our souls speak and carry our bodies like capes.

~ AT THE HOME-ALTAR [1978]

At Betharram

Here a mile down at Betharram
The grottos start winding
Through the earth.
The walls seep
With last year's rain,
And I go down, alone, breathing
An air that's never
Been breathed.

And the farther I go
The more I want it like this in the end –
The earth empty,
My lantern going out in the cold,
The stalactites burning
Like huge wet roots
In the dark.
There's a calm here at Betharram
Deeper than I have ever known.
And down this far,
The heart slows and beats
As calmly as the water
That never stops,
That I hear
Far down in the caves,
Dripping for miles through stone.

⌒ COUNTY O [1984]

At the Olive Grove of the Resistance

He says that home is here,
Here where the earth falls apart
In our hands, and he points
To the one good eye they left him;
Half his world cut out, half
Buried here in the charred roots
Of his three olive trees, four fingers
Down where they made him go
On his knees, his face sliced
To the bone; left him here
To look up and see his oxen
Riding a crown of blood
Into the hills, his trees
Burning, each small olive
Blazing into light; left him
To stumble back up the hill
To find his son face-down

On the stone pathway, his wife
In the shed sprawled on the bags
Of seed, her white breasts
Bruised; left him to wander
Each night in the wind
Born in these black branches,
Or to stand in his small stone room
Spreading the olives out
Like jewels in the sink. And
He tells me the good ones
Go north so he can pay
For the luxury of this light,
The one bare bulb that's the only
flower in his house. And
Because I am new and have come
Here to listen, he cuts one open
And shows me its hard oily pit,
A small black stone that lies here
In his palm, drying in the wind
Brought out of his three olive trees.

Jim Heynen

⁓ A SUITABLE CHURCH [1981]

The Clean People

The clean people worry me.
Wherever I go, I face the glare
of their immaculate smiles,
their polished demeanor
declaring the good life of order.
Where is the smudged
message of grief,
the scuff-marks of pain?
With all the dirt in the world,
who got theirs?

I think I am one
and take my place with the soiled.
We are *the others*
who cannot balance budgets,
nor wear white to our weddings.
Our garb is the haggard
will to survive.
Our language is the mono-
syllabics of dust.
Disorderly, vagrant,
we make our salacious way,
staining the world as we go.
We sing of flesh and the earth,

while they,
haloed in an absence of filth,
must live near God,
their heavenly songs
lodged in the unmarred
keyboards of their grins.

Here they come now,
their clean mouths open,
spilling light as they go.

George Hitchcock

⌒ THE PIANO BENEATH THE SKIN [1978]

Solitaire

all that winter you were gone
the skylarks went on crutches
I woke up every dawn
to crows quarreling in ditches

I'd been there before I knew
that landscape of demented kings
I'd seen the courtiers in blue
masks and idiot posturings

when you're nailed to a scar
you don't think much of fine words
the jugglers at the bazaar
or the man who eats swords

the world's deceptive – too many
crafty smiling bones
eyes masquerading in money
and loquacious spoons

so I said goodbye to the foxtrot
and to badminton in the park
I shuffle the deck and deal out
snowflakes in the dark

Gary H. Holthaus

Unexpected Manna

Those ancient Greeks
Who had a word for everything
Were more articulate than I.

Those Israelites
Who could not spell
The name of God
Are closer kin to me.

Some thing too highly prized
Or close; those that skirt
The edge of pain
Will always be unnamed.

So you,
Falling on my days
Like unexpected manna,
Alter every image
And rearrange my mind
So wholly
I am rendered silent
Gathering in my self
So quietly
That what you do for me
Remains unnamed.

Richard Hugo

⌐ DUWAMISH HEAD [1976]

Neighbor

The drunk who lives across the street from us
fell in our garden, on the beet patch
yesterday. So polite. Pardon me,
he said. He had to be helped up and held,
steered home and put to bed, declaring
we got to have another drink and smile.

I admit my envy. I've found him in salal
and flat on his face in lettuce, and bent
and snoring by that thick stump full of rain
we used to sail destroyers on.
And I've carried him home so often
stone to the rain and me, and cheerful.

I try to guess what's in that dim warm mind.
Does he think about horizoned firs
black against the light, thirty years
ago, and the good girl – what's her name –
believing, or think about the dog
he beat to death that day in Carbonado?

I hear he's dead, and wait now on my porch.
He must be in his shack. The wagon's
due to come and take him where they take
late alcoholics, probably called Farm's End.
I plan my frown, certain he'll be carried out
bleeding from the corners of his grin.

T. E. Jay

~ RIVER DOGS [1976]

Fir

He eats rain
and the shared light
of a single star.

The far-rooted wind
blesses and terrifies him
        in turn.

His slow fire burns greener
than a great cat's eye.
Blind as the sky,
he never sleeps
but his dreams
can make it snow.

Richard Jones

Times Like This

She closes the gate
of the public garden
behind her, an autumn garden,
walled-in, without flowers,
only bare fruit trees
and the intimation
of bad weather.
I'm by myself on the bench,
the leaves, like the children
we talked about having,
racing back and forth
in the windy sunshine
at my feet. It's a scene
we know by heart –
the careful voices,
the careful good-byes.
We've learned it is better
not to talk at times like this
but to leave quietly when
we must, the only sound
the click of a lock.
The afternoon caught
between apple trees
twisted in thought
and pomegranates blooming
along the north wall,
I see she's gone for good.
I count the minutes,
the bricks in the wall,
the money I'll need next week,
the children we won't have.
This small garden

is the perfect size
for my angry heart,
for all the dark words
that created this silence,
for the emptiness
which will survive
in the solitude of desire,
and for the rough grace
which illuminates the soul,
poised between love and nothing.

⌇ AT LAST WE ENTER PARADISE [1991]

The Poet's Heart

Think of the Buddhist monks
who sat in the road
at the start of the war,
saffron robes soaked in gasoline,
and set themselves on fire.

Think of the violence,
the immolation, the composed desire
for peace
silently spoken to ashes;
think of the gift,
the eloquence of their burning.

Poems, too, burn
like a body on fire,
devoted, implacable,
not in flashing epiphany,
but steadily, like the priests
and the world they could imagine.

Think, too, of Shelley's drowned body
burning on the beach in Italy,
of Trelawny, who reached

into the fire
to steal the poet's heart.
The poet's heart:
what the fire could not consume.

~ A PERFECT TIME [1994]

The Novel

   I.

For two days I've been crying,
from Paris to Rome, from Rome to Palermo,
weeping and sobbing here on the train
over a nineteenth-century novel.
Some paragraphs are so beautiful
I lean my head against the window
while villages fly past
like books I'll never open.
When I come to the last few sentences
of an exquisitely painful chapter,
I drop the novel in my lap
or crush it to my chest
and cover my face with my hands,
trembling and shaking.

People on the train
don't know what to do with me
or why I rock back and forth
clutching my book and sniffling.
From Paris to Rome,
the French hated me for crying.
They blew smoke in my face
and cursed me in their beautiful language.
But now, along the Amalfi Coast,
beside blue waters and grottos,
the great hearts of the Italians

take pity –
they offer me water,
offer me wine.

We open the window and smoke together
until I compose myself.
These are my five angels –
a baker from Napoli,
a nun,
young Raphael the fisherman,
and an old married couple,
young lovers once,
now shrunk to the size of children.
The baker from Napoli speaks for them all,
asking what troubles me.
The five Italians lean forward.
For a long moment I'm silent,
looking down at the novel
that is the story of my life,
a secret between the author and me.
I am the hero,
and though I am brave,
indefatigable, loyal, intrepid,
I cannot bear to hear it all again.
My story is blessed with moments of joy,
but they are brief
and flicker like distant stars.
The author knows
truth is tragic.
Relentless, tireless, devoid of sympathy,
he talks and talks
like the heartbeat of time
while I grow weaker and weaker,
no longer a hero,
but a boy again,
weeping when my mother falls ill in the castle,
weeping when Fabiana, my little sister,
is abducted by thieves and gypsies
and forced to dance naked
before a fire in the camp of the Hussars.

The Italians are waiting.
I look up at the luggage rack,
suitcases, and plastic bags
piled precariously over their heads.
I look out the window at blue doors and green doors
of whitewashed houses built on the edges of cliffs
here at the foot of the famous volcano.
When I finally lean forward, I whisper,
slowly, so they will understand,
"My wife died,
and my child,
horribly,
in an accident,
in America, America ,
an accident in America,
my wife and child,
morto, morto,"
The Italians lean back,
overcome, delighted,
crossing themselves,
everyone is talking at once.
My confession makes them happy,
makes them hungry.
They bring out sandwiches,
pears, olives, and cheese.
We feast all afternoon
until sated and sleepy,
until they all lean back in their worn red seats
and the baker, with his hands, asks,
"And now?"
I tell them I'll retreat
to an island to rest,
recover, renew my life
again. I tell this
in broken Italian
and simple French,
using only the present tense and infinitives.
I employ words I remember
from German and Spanish,

I speak English when the story
becomes complex and difficult
though the words themselves
are plain and simple.
My five angels understand best
when I make wild and mysterious gestures
with my hands, when I beat my fist
against the coffin of my heart
or fall silent,
and they have only to look in my face
to see how far I've come,
to see my heart is broken.

II.

As the sun goes down,
I tell them a story,
make them swear never to repeat it,
telling the story only in English
to emphasize feeling over fact.
"I saw something very strange
today in Rome," I tell them.
"I was passing the time between trains
in the gardens of the Villa Borghese,
sitting on a bench, eating ice cream.
A man walked toward me down the gravel path
near the stalls of the *carabinieri*.
Smartly dressed, handsome, he seemed
carefree, tossing keys in his left hand
and humming under the linden trees.
A moment later a woman rushed through the gate,
running toward him,
awkwardly carrying her coat
as her shoulder bag bounced and knocked against her.
She was screaming; he ignored her
and kept walking.
I thought perhaps that he had said something to her
on the street before entering the garden
or had been forward on a crowded bus,

that she came now for revenge,
to defend her honor,
that he would feign innocence,
swear he'd never touched her.
When the woman caught the man,
she dropped her coat and bag,
spun him around
and beat him with her fists,
scratching his face,
clawing his eyes.
And the man did nothing
except close his eyes
and hold on to his broken glasses,
absorbing the blows like a saint,
like a martyr.
It was then I realized
he loved her,
she was his wife,
that she too must have loved him very much
to attack him this way in a public park.
She beat him until there was no good in it,
until he turned away
and, his back to her, began to weep.
She stepped back, yelling,
hurling questions at the wall of his back.
He turned. Unable to meet her eyes,
he said something so softly
only she could hear.
Then she took a step forward,
wanting to hit him again,
raised her fists,
but fury had left her
and the man walked away
down the path in sorrow.
She followed,
but not before she bent to pick up
the keys he had dropped in the dirt,
the keys he would have forgotten
and lost
had she not been there."

I ask the Italians if they understand.
No one says a word. Now,
I tell them, I will finish the story,
this parable, this little novel,
reminding them of their vow
never to repeat it.

"The man and woman walked to the stables
where they studied the horses of the *carabinieri*.
The proud horses – usually aloof and haughty –
returned the lovers' gaze with patient brown eyes,
tossing their heads sympathetically
like priests.
               And though I had no right
to follow the lovers with my ice cream and notebook,
though the lovers' novel was written in Italian,
I eavesdropped as the horses spoke,
as horses in Italian novels sometimes do,
forgiving the man his infidelity,
the woman her inability to forgive.
The horse-priests said,
La passione è difficile,
and offered themselves
as models of discipline.
The horses said their lives were a novel
full of grain and wind and sweat.
They told of men in blue uniforms
who arrive with the light each dawn
to wash and brush them,
bringing fresh straw.
The horses said they love each day,
galloping through the woods
or walking slowly by the villa's open windows
so their riders can admire the lovely sculptures,
the horrible *Rape of Persephone*,
the terrible *Apollo and Daphne*.
The horses said they don't understand
the human love
of stories in marble and bronze.
They understand only

that each day as they enter the woods
with light falling through trees
with leaves under their hooves,
their hearts become so full they think
if they don't die right then
they will surely live forever.
And when the horses fell silent
and bent their heads to the sweet water
flowing fresh down the long wooden trough,
the lovers turned away,
perhaps toward home,
where they would make love,
touching each other gently with respect,
then with increasing passion and need,
healing one another simply
with their love."

In the compartment,
the baker, nun, fisherman,
and tiny old couple
listen to each word,
leaning forward when I whisper,
nodding at a word they understand –
carabinieri, Bernini.
But I am finished talking;
I will say nothing more in English.
But they don't know that yet,
and watch me and wait to see if the story continues.
When I finally lower my head,
open my book
and continue reading,
they don't wait for my tears;
they argue over the meaning of my story,
yelling at one another,
waving hands, interpreting,
translating, revising, editing, embellishing,
digressing
into the mystery
of lives they have observed,
adding their own emotions

and personal histories
as if they've comprehended everything I've said
and no longer need to consult me,
talking among themselves now
as if I had disappeared.

III.

Just before midnight,
we take turns in the w.c.
with our toothbrushes and our washcloths.
When the coach lights go out,
the nun vows to watch over me
as I finish my book by flashlight,
but she's a tired angel
and falls asleep in a minute.
The old couple curl
on their seats like two cats –
they're that small.
The baker snorts and snores,
hands on belly,
face white as flour in the moonlight.
But Raphael, the fisherman,
is too young to sleep.
He stands outside in the corridor,
admiring the moon and moonlit water,
thinking,

I will tell my friends
what I heard and saw on my journey.
I will sit in my uncle's café
and my cousin will bring wine and glasses.
We'll drink to the moon
bathing the rocky coast of our village
and to spells the moon casts on fish
we catch in our nets at dawn.
I will tell my friends about the strange American
and how fine it is to stay up all night
admiring the moon,
admiring the moonlit water.

And I will tell them how,
when the entire train was dreaming
except for the American
hidden behind his book and flashlight,
I saw an old man in the next compartment
sitting across from his daughter,
admiring her as she slept,
tenderly, secretly watching her,
biting his knuckle now and then,
so astonished was he by her beauty.

The Key

This is the key to my happiness,
the key to my room
in the *Hôtel du Paradis.*
The tireless Algerian
keeps the keys behind the bar all day
to return to me at midnight
when I climb the narrow, winding stairs
with my pounding heart and loneliness.
The Algerian calls out *bonne nuit*;
I struggle with the broken lock.
A flimsy door, I could kick it down,
but when I am patient,
when, in my quietest voice,
I say *please*
it opens
and lets me in.
I turn on the light
and there is the cell of my dreary room –
the unmade bed, the open suitcase,
pitcher of stale water on the table.
I unlatch the window
and lean into the night
above torches of countless street lamps
and wild cars carving the boulevards
with blades of rushing lights.
I pray to the moon

rising above dark steeples,
ask the moon to translate for stars
listening unseen
beyond the city's dazzling lights.
Night after night,
sitting in my window, hungry and tired,
or pacing back and forth before my desk,
I have come to love
the one dim bulb
dangling from the ceiling on a thin black cord.
I have come to trust
the smallest illumination,
the tiniest omen,
wallpaper peeling away
to reveal origins and mysteries,
the hotel's ten thousand ghosts
and the sickly-sweet perfume of their bodies.
I've learned to write or read
to the music of motorcycles
roaring down tangled streets
or to fall asleep
long after midnight
to singing on sidewalks below.
Locking my door,
I turn out the light
to the distant wailing of sirens,
sit on my bed and consider my key,
a silver key with a worn yellow tag
the yellow of a dying daffodil,
room number 8 in red,
symbol of infinity
and my lucky number.
I've begun to believe
in the numerology of my birth –
August 8th, '53 –
three 8's in a row,
three affirmations
I will live forever.
I put the key under my pillow,
lie down,

cross my arms on my chest
and feel my beating heart
promising everything
if only I can wait until morning
when I wake
to the wild music
of all the city's church bells,
when I open my door
and lock it behind me,
when I bound down the winding stairs
that rush to the street,
to flower shops and cafés,
to the parks and river
and every stranger waiting
to ask my name
and greet me with a kiss –
all this,
my heart promises,
tomorrow,
after I've turned out the light
and slept on the narrow bed,
after I've awakened
and returned the key
to the smiling Algerian,
who waits behind the bar each morning
with my hunk of bread and my coffee,
my sugar and my cream.

Jean Joubert

⌒ BLACK IRIS [1988]

Brilliant Sky

Never between the branches has the sky
burned with such brilliance, as if
it were offering all of its light to me,
to say – what? what urgent mystery
strains at that transparent mouth?
No leaf, no rustle . . . It's in winter,
in cold emptiness and silence, that the air
suddenly arches itself like this into infinity,
and glitters.
            This evening, far from here,
a friend is entering his death,
he knows it, he walks
under bare trees alone,
perhaps for the last time. So much love,
so much struggle, spent and worn thin.
But when he looks up, suddenly the sky
is arrayed in this same vertiginous clarity.

Translated from the French by Denise Levertov

Jaan Kaplinski

⌒ THE WANDERING BORDER [1987]

"We started home, my son and I"

We started home, my son and I.
Twilight already. The Young moon
stood in the western sky and beside it
a single star. I showed them to my son
and explained how the moon should be greeted
and that this star is the moon's servant.
As we neared home, he said
that the moon is far, as far
as that place where we went.
I told him the moon is much, much farther
and reckoned: if one were to walk
ten kilometers each day, it would take
almost a hundred years to reach the moon.
But this was not what he wanted to hear.
The road was already almost dry.
The river was spread on the marsh; ducks and other waterfowl
crowed the beginning of night. The snow's crust
crackled underfoot – it must
have been freezing again. All the houses' windows
were dark. Only in our kitchen
a light shone. Beside our chimney, the shining moon,
and beside the moon, a single star.

Translated from the Estonian by the author with Sam Hamill and Riina Tamm

Shirley Kaufman

⌒ RIVERS OF SALT [1993]

By the Rivers

That spring he was fourteen,
sun on the walls, stale air
sweet in Bergen-Belsen for the first time,
he told me he thought of the nurse
who held him when he was small.
He found a corner
where they did not catch him:
rush of the brilliance and the heat
and no one there. He opened his clothes,
hunched over his wasted body,
and made it spill.

*

The poem wants to look forward, not
back, but out there as far as it can see
are ruins: body of Abel body of god body
of smoke. And no recognizable
child to mourn.

So it begins with longing.
Or with fear, that old dog
stinking beside it, scabby and blind.

And all the time the future
is pushing up uncalled for
under the cold ground, or gliding down
like the first snow, wet syllables
that melt and soak up darkness.

The poem wants to get out of
where it is. But is instructed
to remember. In shameless daylight.
By the rivers of salt.

~ ROOTS IN THE AIR: NEW AND SELECTED POEMS [1996]

The Accuser

The knife was much sharper than I thought,
and severed the head. I was relieved
it stayed on her neck, although
she was bleeding across the throat
and down the shoulders from under
the bun. The whole body
stood where it was, accusing.

Sometimes in dreams she comes back
shaking her finger, whatever I did
I didn't. As if bewildered
by my anger, comes back
out of the twilight as the trees
darken there on our front porch,
her eyes from a Russian novel.

She caresses the scar on her throat
like a string of worry beads,
calling, *you'll catch your death,*
as if it were butterflies
or fish, *this time you'll be sorry,*
all the years of my childhood calling,
still calling me home.

The Buddha of Sŏkkuram

In the silence
all extremes are alike
  – Roberto Juarroz

When light burns from the sea
to the mountain and the jewel
in the Buddha's white granite forehead
catches fire, the sun
plows everything silver.

He's looking at nothing,
his eyes are closed

the way we distance ourselves
to see more clearly.

Stone hushed against stone,
he's done with the welling up
and the ebbing

as in the Pietà, the forebearance
even of the toes
worn down and kissed into brightness.

          *

If you follow the Kyŏngju road
to the bottom of the hill
where the kings are buried

you come to a huge black tulip
turned over. The bell
wouldn't ring when they cast it
so they melted it down
and threw a child in the molten bronze.

The dragon was appeased.

How big a fire does it take
for a small soul?

Or for a small girl's body
to burn away from its cry
until only the cry lasts
out of the hollow where her ribs were
calling her mother

if we believe such stories.
That was twelve hundred years ago.
Nobody strikes it now.

　　　*

History is a reversible rug we turn over
when the colors fade.
It lies with its face to the floor
so that we let it happen to others
or in art.

　　　What can I do
with the dailiness of shock,
mute as the etching of a woman
holding her dead child,

its almost fluorescent head fallen back
as if the neck were broken,
bones of her hand as in an x-ray
mapping her pain.

Light blooms from the body
of a child, its weightless presence,
and a woman who knows about loss
far into the future.

Her lap supporting the infant
is a Buddha's lap.

　　　*

I keep trying to put them
together

      his weightless shoulders
and the silenced bell

color of morning on the stone
like light returning
to the skin of my body
when I wake

or the rim of the glass
beside my bed.
Even to emptiness

        or grief
sliding down his right arm
where the hand rests easy across the leg
down the other
finger by finger
over his silky foot.

Poem in November

Past the fierce Guardians
with their swollen scowls, past
the Great Southern Gate,
behind the bronze Buddha there's a test
for getting to Paradise.
Not sure if they're losers or winners
skinny children line up
and squirm on their bellies
through the hole at the base of a pillar.
One of them is stuck in the middle,
her shoulders won't budge.
Friends push from behind
where her feet thrash, others tug
at her arms until she emerges
red-faced and crying.

Not ready for Paradise, not even
tested, not wanting to lose
the heat of my body, I jog
until my breath slams at my ribs.
Leaves are flying all over the gardens,
tiny fans of the gingkos
spread themselves open and flutter
for the last time, yellow on yellow,
lit-up, as if they have to be
luminous at the end.

At the women's college they're modeling
old kimonos to American rap.
The loose sleeves billow to the beat
of the music. I learn to suck noodles
through my closed lips, and they smile
with approval cheerfully coaxing
their grandmother to eat. Their teacher
whose name means cedar mountain
was a child in Nagasaki before the bomb.
"Even a lion does not eat a lion,"
he says so softly I can hardly hear
the swell of his old grief under the small
syllables and the immeasurable emptiness.
He sighs like the steppes of Asia.
"We don't say *life-and-death*
in our language," he tells me standing
on his kitchen balcony. Sheaves of rice
are hung out to dry. He shows me
the cut stalks. "We say *death-and-life*."

Pressed against the dark rail of the war
refusing to be reminded or to forget,
I look at the buds still wrapped
on the ripening kernels. I want
to be in there, unhatched and unpolished.

There are people who sit in the malls
all day in their incompleteness
gripping the handles of desire.

Something is riding on their hunched backs,
clawing their shoulders. When they shoot
the balls madly into their slots,
neon lit marbles, little joy-
rides to nowhere,
they are shaking it off.

That's my face wrinkled in the pond
among the hundred-year-old carp.
They drift fat and golden
through the lotus. Sometimes
I wake up lying on an x-ray table
inhaling deeply, letting it out.
Strapped between my skin and the surface
of things, gold leaf and lacquer
and the lumpish flesh, I'm waiting
for the bad news.

          If I am happy
in the carefully raked gardens, the studied
random balance of crane and turtle
and fifteen positioned rocks,
or in our bare room where we've fallen
between the futons, light seeping
through the screen, holding
and being held, and if I'm glad
when water flows down the face of the granite
into its bamboo channel
the way it was meant to, is it because
I don't trust the unexpected
I used to want more of? Am I resigned
to safety? Brimming unseen in the green scrub,
the bamboo sōzu empties with a sharp crack
frightening the deer.

"Every rock has a being of its own."
The priest says he worked as a bank clerk
until he was fifty. Not wanting
his emptiness but mine, I try
to be still again the way I learned it

in the sixties. I try not to try.
To hear the leaves. This one,
for instance. The wind nudged it
from the maple as I raised my head
and already it's a lost thought,
all the colors are sailing past me.
Not the rock. How stony it is!
And weathered, like the old poems.
Tilted a little to one side
but not unbalanced.

Masako says her mother took the train
to Nara with her haiku club
to watch the full moon on the rippled sand.
What does an old woman do
with the moon in her hair all night?
What does she hear in the bright dark
when she listens to the sound
of no water under the sand?

Kawamura Yoichi

⁓ LIKE UNDERGROUND WATER [1995]

On the Sand Dune

Holding a keepsake of the wind in its hand,
a figure stands in silence.
Is it my shadow, wearing black algae?

When I shout, it's spring; when I pray, it's summer;
when I look back, it's autumn.
Is that winter holding white hair in its hands?

The sound of gunfire passes over the dark sand dune.
Who is it, scattering breaths of death
over the estuary of flames?

A legend concerning me has it
that I roamed through palm tree woods with raw *sake* in my hands,
turning my back on the sound of gunfire and the voices of women.

We no longer have love songs of the *Manyō*.
A heavy rain wets down the times of antiquity.
Everything is blown away by the wind through the riverbed.

Therefore, wind,
run through me at top speed, piercing me
under the broken, majestic chandelier.

Translated from the Japanese by Naoshi Koriyama and Edward Lueders

NOTE: The *Manyō* is the eighth-century Japanese anthology.

Ki Joon

THE MOONLIT POND: KOREAN CLASSICAL POEMS IN CHINESE [1997]

Elegy for Myself

When the sun sets, the sky is inky dark;
Deep in the mountains, the ravine is cloudy.
All the human wishes retained for a thousand years
Are finally fulfilled by a single mound.

Translated from the Chinese by Sung-Il Lee

Carolyn Kizer

Bitch

Now, when he and I meet, after all these years,
I say to the bitch inside me, don't start growling.
He isn't a trespasser anymore,
Just an old acquaintance tipping his hat.
My voice says, "Nice to see you,"
As the bitch starts to bark hysterically.
He isn't an enemy now,
Where are your manners, I say, as I say,
"How are the children? They must be growing up."
At a kind word from him, a look like the old days,
The bitch changes her tone: she begins to whimper.
She wants to snuggle up to him, to cringe.
Down, girl! Keep your distance
Or I'll give you a taste of the choke-chain.
"fine, I'm just fine," I tell him.
She slobbers and grovels.
After all, I am her mistress. She is basically loyal.
It's just that she remembers how she came running
Each evening, when she heard his step;
How she lay at his feet and looked up adoringly
Though he was absorbed in his paper;
Or, bored with her devotion, ordered her to the kitchen
Until he was ready to play.
But the small careless kindnesses
When he'd had a good day, or a couple of drinks,
Come back to her now, seem more important
Than the casual cruelties, the ultimate dismissal.
"It's nice to see you are doing so well," I say.
He couldn't have taken you with him;
You were too demonstrative, too clumsy,

Not like the well-groomed pets of his new friends.
"Give my regards to your wife," I say. You gag
As I drag you off by the scruff,
Saying, "Goodbye! Goodbye! Nice to have seen you again."

For Sappho / After Sappho

1.

and you sang eloquently
for my pleasure
before I knew
you were girl or boy

    at the moment
    dawn awoke me
    you were in my bed

not sister   not lover
fierce though you were
a small cat
with thorny claws

    any daughter
    seeking comfort

you asked what you could give
to one whom you thought
possessed everything

    then you forgot giving
    and tried to take
    blindly seeking the breast

what to do but hold you
lost innocent . . .

we love whatever
caresses us
in need or pleasure
a debt a favor
a desperation

you were already
a speaking instrument
I loved the speaker
loved the voice
as it broke my heart with pity

    breath immortal
    the words nothing
    articulate poems
    not pertinent   the breath
    everything

you the green shoot
I the ripe earth
alas not yours

    2.

the punch bowl was full
a boy flirted
in our drunken dance
you dripped sweat
trembling shook your body
you tried to kill him
black darts shot from your eyes

    and the company laughed
    at your desperation

someone took you away
you lay on the grass
retching   then spewed your love
over the bed of crocus buds

we led you home
where I confronted
your mother's picture
my face enameled

I have a slender daughter
a golden flower
your eyes are dark as olive pits
not for me to devour
child   no child of mine

you screamed after me
Aphrodite! not giving
as with a sweep of my cloak
I fled skyward ...

the full moon is shining
in the spring twilight
your face more pallid
than dry grass
and vomit-stained
still you are the evening star

most beautiful star
you will die a virgin

Aphrodite
thick-armed and middle-aged
loving the love of men
yet mourns you

3.

when I lost you
where did you go
only the fragments of your poems
mourn you as I mourn you

and the unwritten poems leapt with you
over the cliffside

hyacinth hair   rising
in the rush of wind

hyacinth shattered
a dark stain on the ground
yet wine   some drops
some essence
has been distilled

this mouth drinks thirstily
as it chokes on the dust of your death

4.

yet I hold you in midair
androgynous child of dream
offshoot of muses

my thought holds you
straight-browed and piercing-eyed
breastless as a boy
as light of foot

wandering in the world
beyond this   and before

but for now you forget it all
in Lethe
I too am treacherous   I forget everything
mind and limbs loosen
in the arms of a stranger
searching for Lethe

but you dart through the future
which is memory
your boy's voice shouting out
the remainder of poems
of which I know
simply beginnings

words heard a thousand times
in the echoing night
across the sea-foam

separating us
for this moment only

IN MEMORIAM: S. L. M. B.

⌒ THE NEARNESS OF YOU [1986]

Thrall

The room is sparsely furnished:
A chair, a table and a father.

He sits in the chair by the window.
There are books on the table.
The time is always just past lunch.

You tiptoe past as he eats his apple
And reads. He looks up, angry.
He has heard your asthmatic breathing.

He will read for years without looking up
Until your childhood is over:

Smells, untidiness and boring questions;
Blood, from the first skinned knees
To the first stained thighs;
The foolish tears of adolescent love.

One day he looks up, pleased
At the finished product.
Now he is ready to love you!

So he coaxes you in the voice reserved
For reading Keats. You agree to everything.

Drilled in silence and duty,
You will give him no cause for reproach.
He will boast of you to strangers.

When the afternoon is older
Shadows in a smaller room
Fall on the bed, the books, the father.

You read aloud to him
"La Belle Dame sans Merci."
You feed him his medicine.
You tell him you love him.

You wait for his eyes to close at last
So you may write this poem.

~ CARRYING OVER: POEMS FROM THE CHINESE, URDU,
MACEDONIAN, YIDDISH, AND FRENCH AFRICAN [1988]

Brother, I Am Here

Coolness, like the evening tide,
Covers, one by one, the steps of the twisting trail
And slips into your heart.
You sit on the threshold
Of the dismal shack that squats behind you.
Like birds, leaves drift from the locust trees
And little moon-coins float
On the ripple of waves.

You belonged to the sun, the prairie,
The dikes, the world of amorous jewel-black eyes.
The you belonged to the hurricane,
To the route, the torches, the arms
Supporting each other.
Soldier, your life was plangent as a bell
Shaking the shadows from the human heart.

Now the wind steals away with alien steps;
It refuses to believe
That you are melancholy still.

But I am with you, Brother,
And the newsstand, the park benches, the apple cores
Revive in your recollection
With smiles and lamps and delicate rhythms.

Then they glide away on the lines of the writing paper.

Only when the night wind
Shifts the direction of your thoughts,
Only when that trumpet of yours
Is suddenly silent, craving echoes,
I shall be back (with hope alive)
Calmly at your side, to say
Brother, I am here.

Translated from the Chinese of Shu Ting

~ HARPING ON: POEMS 1985–1995 [1996]

Election Day, 1984

Did you ever see someone cold-cock a blind nun?
Well, I did. Two helpful idiots
Steered her across the tarmac to her plane
And led her smack into the wing.
She deplaned with two black eyes and a crooked wimple,
Bruised proof that the distinction is not simple
Between ineptitude and evil.
Today, with the President's red button playing
Such a prominent role,
Though I can't vote for it, I wonder
If evil could be safer, on the whole.

On a Line from Valéry

THE GULF WAR

Tout le ciel vert se meurt
Le dernier arbe brûle.

The whole green sky is dying. The last tree flares
With a great burst of supernatural rose
Under a canopy of poisonous airs.

Could we imagine our return to prayers
To end in time before time's final throes,
The green sky dying as the last tree flares?

But we were young in judgement, old in years
Who could make peace; but it was war we chose,
To spread its canopy of poisoning airs.

Not all our children's pleas and women's fears
Could steer us from this hell. And now God knows
His whole green sky is dying as it flares.

Our crops of wheat have turned to fields of tares.
This dreadful century staggers to its close
And the sky dies before us, its poisoned heirs.

All rain was dust. Its granules were our tears.
Throats burst as universal winter rose
To kill the whole green sky, the last tree bare
Beneath its canopy of poisoned air.

William Kloefkorn

Why the Stone Remains Silent

1.

It wants to say something,
it wants more than almost anything
to speak its mind.
Since the rise of the first Caesar
it has been layering itself,
each fine flake the budding
of a thick compacted tongue.

Yet it remains silent,
waiting for the precise moment.
It has been advised by an oracle
that, having spoken, it might never
ever be able to speak again.
At one time, watching Attila
with his clubhead poised,
it was sorely tempted.
Auschwitz, another.
But it remained silent,
and is silent today,
waiting for the proper moment.

2.

Thus season after season
we plow and plant around it:
plow and plant, plant and harvest,
harvest and plow
around it.
Yet it remains silent.
We see it unmoved, and we tell ourselves

we understand:
it awaits that most propitious moment.

And more than understand, we worship:
praise to the stone,
all glory to the silence at the center of the stone,
to the budding of its thick compacted tongue,
to the wise, heavy heart engorged with mercy,
that has the power, but lacks the will,
to put an end to indeterminate suffering.

Kwon P'il

⁓ THE MOONLIT POND: KOREAN CLASSICAL POEMS IN CHINESE
[1997]

Alone at Night

The way of the world as it is,
What can I do about the fleeting time?
As a few chrysanthemums shiver in the late autumn,
Cricket chirps grow louder as the night deepens.
The sad moon throws its beams on the windowpanes;
And wind shakes the rustling branches.
Recalling what has happened over the last ten years,
I sit before a lamp, counting the moths flying into it.

Translated from the Chinese by Sung-Il Lee

James Laughlin

~ THE OWL OF MINERVA [1987]

O Best of All Nights, Return and Return Again

How she let her long hair down over her shoulders, making a love
    cave around her face. Return and return again.
How when the lamplight was lowered she pressed against him,
    twining her fingers in his. Return and return again.
How their legs swam together like dolphins and their toes played
    like little tunnies. Return and return again.
How she sat beside him cross-legged, telling him stories of her
    childhood. Return and return again.
How she closed her eyes when his were open, how they breathed
    together, breathing each other. Return and return again.
How they fell into slumber, their bodies curled together like
    two spoons. Return and return again.
How they went together to Otherwhere, the fairest land they had
    ever seen. Return and return again.
O best of all nights, return and return again.

(*After the* Pervigilium Veneris *&* Propertius's "*Nox Mihi Candia*")

⌢ THE BIRD OF ENDLESS TIME [1989]

My Ambition

is to become a footnote
in a learned work of the

22nd century   not just a
"cf" or a "see" but a sol-

id note such as Raby gives
Walafrid Strabo in *Christ-*

ian Latin Poetry or Ernst
Robert Curtius (the most

erudite German who ever
lived) devotes to Alber-

tino Mussato in his *Euro-*
päische Literatur und La-

teinisches Mittelalter   I
hope the scholar of the

22nd will lick his schol-
arly lips when he finds me

in some forgotten source
(perhaps the *Obloquies* of

Dreadful Edward Dahlberg)
and think here is an odd-

ball I would have liked
immortalizing me in six

turgid lines of footnote.

David Lee

For Jan, with Love

1.

John he comes to my house
pulls his beat up truck in my drive
and honks
Dave John sez Dave my red sow
she got pigs stuck and my big hands they wont go
and I gotta get them pigs out
or that fucker shes gonna die
and I sez John goddam
well be right down and John sez Jan
he yells JAN wheres Jan shes got little hands
she can get in there and pull them pigs
and I sez Jan and he sez Jan and Jan comes
what? Jan sez and John sez tell Jan Dave
and I sez Jan Johns red sows got pigs
stuck and his hands too big and wont go
and hes gotta get them pigs out
or that fuckers gonna die (John he turns
his head and lights a cigarette)
(he dont say fuck to no woman)
and Jan she sez well lets go
and we get in Johns beat up damn truck
and go to pull Johns pigs

2.

Johns red sow she doesn't weigh
a hundred and sixty pounds
but he bred her to his biggest boar
and had to put hay bales by her sides
so the boar wouldn't break

her back because Carl bet five dollars
he couldnt and John he bet
five she could and John he won
but Carl enjoyed watching anyway

   3.

Johns red sow was laying
on her side hurting bad
and we could see she had a pig
right there but it wouldnt come she
was too small and John sez see
and I sez I see that pigs gotta come out
or that fuckers gonna die
and Jan puts vaseline on her hands
and sez hold her legs and I hold her legs
and Jan goes in after the pig
and John gets out of the pen and goes
somewheres else

Jan she pulls like hell pretty soon
the pig come big damn big little pig
dead and I give Jan more vaseline and she goes
back to see about any more
and Johns red sow pushes hard on Jans arm
up to her elbow inside and Jan sez
theres more help me and I help
another pig damn big damn dead comes
and Johns red sow she seems better
and we hope thats all

   4.

Johns red sow wont go
out of labor so we stay all night
and John brings coffee and smokes
and flashlight batteries and finally Jan
can feel another pig but Johns red sows
swole up tight and she cant grab hold
but only touch so I push her side

and she grunts and screams and shits all over Jans arm
and Jan sez I got it help me and I help
and we pull for a goddam hour and pull
the pigs head off

and I sez oh my god we gotta get that pig now
or that fuckers gonna die for sure
and John sez what happened? and Jan
gives him a baby pigs head in his hand
and John goes somewheres else again
while Jan goes back fast inside
grabbing hard and Johns red sow
hurts bad and Jan sez I got something help me
and I help and we start taking that pig out
piece by piece.

    5.

Goddamn you bitch dont you die
Jan yells when Johns red sow dont help no more
and we work and the sun comes up
and we finally get the last piece of pig out
and give Johns red sow a big shot of penicillin
her ass swole up like a football
but she dont labor and John sez
is that all? and Jan wipes her bloody arms
on a rag and sez yes and John climbs in
the pen and sez hows my red sow?
and we look and go home and go to bed
because Johns red sow that fucker she died

⁓ DRIVING & DRINKING [1979]

from Driving & Drinking

. . . This all happened before
I went to work for the lectric company
I was younger and hired on for the oil
oh I made good money and it wasn't bad work

I don't think I'd do it again
anyways we's in Texas up on that panhandle
and had a rig drilling about 8 mile
outa town. We'd work 36 on and 12 off
at least I would cause I could make so much
I'd run chain awhile and then crownest
it never made no different
I was just after the paycheck on Fridays
I'd do about anything they wanted as long
as the money kept coming in and they
seemed to like that
so anyways we was down over a mile
dam near 7 fousand foot
and we knew the oil was right there
we had to be coming thu any time
you just get the feeling it's gonna blow
so here comes the foman cause we sent for him
cause he has to sez when we can cap off
to get ready for the last push thu
so we don't blow all to hell and mebbe catch fire
that foman he's so goddam drunk
he caint tell shit from dog puke
he starts raising all kind of hell saying
you get this dam rig running right NOW
we won't hit no fucking oil
for 2 weeks nobody paid you to think
that what I'm by god paid for
you just drill till I say stop and then
you just ast how long that's all
now git back to goddam work and stop
trying to set round fucking off
he left and we's so mad we couldn't see straight
for a man to talk to us that way
whether he's drunk or not didn't matter
so we set the bit back down in the night
and let her go wot the fuck
and about midnight the crewboss he sez to me
John you go up to the crownest we lifting
that pipe out I aint getting blowed up
for nobody and that was fine by me
we's all getting scairt to where we's just working

and not saying nothing just thinking
bout how long fore morning or till we got off
it's funny how you think the day'll take
the being scairt away but it never really does
anyways I climbt up the derrick to the top
and we's getting ready to pull that pipe out
when all of a sudden the whole thing starts shaking
to where I'm bout to get slung off
and I can hear the crewboss yelling
get down git DOWN this fucker's gonna blow
and by god I burnt the palms off my hands
coming down I slid the wire guy rope
to the platform and then jumped off on the ground
the rest of the crew's arredy running ahead
so's I try to catch up and then I hear
that big sonofabitch touch off K-BOOM
right behint me and caught on fire
it blew me down on the ground and started
me burning by god I was scairt
I jumped up and started running and I'd of
burnt to death if this nigger hadn't grapt me
and thowed me down in this ditch and
put the fire out on my clothes
so's we look and that whole rig's burning
and we can see 2 guys from the crew laying
tween us and the rig burning up
and we know they's dead and
the rest of us is burnt bad where we might die
the crewboss he takes off running
into the fire and he can see he's gonna
try to bring the pickup out
he goes to it and grabs the doorhandle
and it's so hot part of his hand
sticks to the door and just comes off
but he gets in and somehows
he gets that dam truck started and drives out
of that fire I won't never know how
all the wires was burnt up
it got so hot that that truck's paint as all
scorcht off to where you couldn't tell even
what kind of truck it was

and he brings it to us and we get in
I'm so burnt they had to put me in the back
and I'm laying in this feller's lap
who put out the fire in my clothes
and we pull out of there driving like hell
to get to town and by then the fire
was so hot it burnt up the whole goddam rig
there wasn't nothing left and I
seen it bend over just like it was plastic
I wanted to pass out so bad I couldn't stand it
but I didn't I just laid there and felt it all
and saw it all so's we're going to town
as fast as we can go and pass this law
and he turns on his red light and chases us
till he gets close to see and then
he pulls ahead and leads us thu town
about 90 mile a hour to the hospital
where he jumps out and runs over and opens
the door and he just puked like hell
3 up front was arredy dead 2 of them
stuck together they's burnt so bad
and the crewboss's hand was off and he
didn't have no face left
how he drove God knows I don't
and there was only 1 other still alive and
he died that night so then they come
to get us out of the back and they started to lift me
out I sez get him first he saved my life
the man sez it's too late he's done dead
and I was laying in his lap

the onliest 2 that made it was me and
the crewboss. He was in the hospital for
96 days and I was in for 104
a week and a day more
I member cause he come to see me
when they let him out
he was burnt so bad I couldn't tell
who he was till he sed something
he ast if I's okay and I sed yas
we just looked at each other for a minute

and then he walked off
I sez be seeing you be he just waved
3 days later he drove his car
into a bridge and killed hisself
they buried him exactly 1 week after they
let him out and then let me out
the next day after his funeral was over

I don't have no bad scars left that show
my legs is burnt good
but I still feel it I get cold
and have to wear them long underwears
all year long on my legs
and my hands is so thin they bleed easy
my skin's bout as thick as a cigarette paper
and I don't have no feelings in my face
but I'm lucky I guess . . .

⁓ THE PORCINE CANTICLES [1984]

Jan's Birthday

I saved seventy dollars to buy Jan a present
this time because I forgot last year
and went to town to see what I could find.
I found John and he bought a round
and I bought a round and John sez
let's go watch the auction and we drank another beer
and got in my truck and bought a sixpack
and went. They ran a pureblood
spotted poland china sow in and John sez
that's a good one and the man sez who'll start this
at thirty and I felt good about remembering
Jan's birthday and said I will and he started
auctioning but nobody bid and John sez
hope she makes you a nice hog Dave
and I told the man upstairs about Jan's
birthday while he made out the ticket
but he didnt hear and John sez give her to Jan

and she cost sixty-four dollars and ninety-six cents
and after the beer I had thirty-eight cents left
when we loaded up that spotted sow.

I was mad and John sez give her to Jan Dave again
and he bought another beer and I drove
my truck to Woolworth's and went in with my beer
in my hand and bought thirty-eights cents
worth of red ribbon and the lady tied a bow
and gave me a piece of paper so I wrote
For Jan, With Love and John held the spotted sow
by the leg and I tied the ribbon with the bow
around her neck while the lady watched
and said oh my god over and over
the sow screaming like hell stopping cars
and the sheriff drove up and said we had to move
because we were impeding traffic so I pinned the note
to the ribbon and said you gonna help me?
and John sez no I got work to do but you
been to college you'll think of something
so I drove John to his truck
stole two of his beers got drunk
and hit a Piute Indian who hit me back
and a man called the sheriff who sez goddam Dave
and he sez I gotta get out of town or he'll arrest me
and I say Ira I can't drive I'm drunk and Jan will kill me
because it's her birthday and Ira said goddamn Dave again
made me sit in the back with the hog
and a deputy named Melvin drove his car to my house
behind us with the red light flashing
while Ira drove me and Jan's seventy-dollar
happy birthday present home.

~ DAY'S WORK [1990]

Hired Hand

You need some help
out to your place for anything?
What John? I sed
It's a man come around
looking for work
here and there he don't charge much
name Norman and he's willing
to work for money

you cain't get no good help
I hired this one college boy
to help me put sheetiron
on my barn roof
that didn't work out
I told him look
I'm gone splain this one time
and did what I wanted him to do
but ever time he walked by
that pile of sheetiron
he'd stand there combing his hair
in the reflection of it
trying to look purdy
all I had out there was me
and them ewes
I could take a chance on it
whatall might be on his mind
I had to work and the ewes
was arredy bred up
I let him go that day

Norman ain't too smart
but he ain't purdy
and don't worry about it
him and a rooster
could stand there and stare

at a line you drawn
in the dirt with your foot
half the morning till you shook him
but if you tell him
what to do and check up on him
he'll get it done
all of us working together
I imagine we can finish it
before wintertime comes
but he can come help out
over to your place too
I suspicion if you need help
but he ain't much conversation
he just understands
whichever you tell him to do
you shouldn't ask him
for anything more than that
that's all you're paying him for

⌒ MY TOWN [1995]

Benediction

Ellis Britton was standing outside the churchhouse
after the closing prayer by hisself this oncet
you couldn't be there by him and say something
you never known what he would say out loud
he'd goddam this and ohjesustchrist anothern
everbody talking to each other listening
wondering why they didn't go ahead and kick him out
he never put no money in the collection plate anyway
but they known if they did
he'd burn the churchhouse down that night
and their house too if he thought they's in on it
this one time the Campbellites across the street
hadn't quite got done and come out to stare yet
was singing the closing song right before the prayer
come to the line

will there be any stars in my crown?
Ellis he turnt round hollered loud as he could
through their front door open cause it was summer
   no not one
   not a fucking one
wasn't nothing nobody could do
but get in their car and drive off home
one man Lovard Peacock I think back then
about torn his 5 year old boy's shoulder out its socket
pulling him to the parking lot to get away
so nobody would think he sed it
when them Churchofchristers come out to see
only ones left was the Brittons and the preacher
cars pulling out of there like it was Indianapolis
Ellis Britton he grapt his wife by the arm
sed let's get the hell out of here
we don't have to put up with this one bit
that preacher was so embarrassed
he had to go across the street and apologize
to all them Campbellites standing there
so they wouldn't think he was responsible
for Ellis Britton saying such a terrible thing
even if it might of been true

so this one day I'm talking about
that preacher didn't want to be polite
he walked up to Ellis Britton over off by hisself
had to find the right thing to say so Ellis
wouldn't have something to thrown a fit about
the whole congregation standing there listening to see
sed Brother Britton your wife sure is looking nice today
Ellis Britton sed oh bullshit
she's so goddamn fat won't none of her clothes
fit her no more
she gets up a sweat even thinking
about walking outside to get the mail
it soaks in to the furniture
where it smells like hogs been in heat wallering on it
you caint even stand to set there
it'll slime up your clothes so bad

your britches climb up in the crack of your ast
and stick the rest of the day
you have to peel it out at night
I believe she's the second fattest womern in the churchhouse
she caint find no clothes to buy in this town
even her underwears is too tight
the rubbers won't stretch enough
and it leaves a dent all night on her belly
they don't make them big enuf that we can find
so what I want to know Reverent
is whar does your wife go to buy her drawers?
by god if they can fit her
they ought to be able to have some for my Lorene
that preacher learnt his lesson that day
after that he let Ellis Britton stand by hisself studying sidewalks
outside the churchhouse when the services was over
just like everbody else had learned how to do before he come along

Denise Levertov

Poet and Person

I send my messages ahead of me.
You read them, they speak to you
in siren tongues, ears of flame
spring from your heads to take them.

When I arrive, you love me,
for I sing those messages you've
learned by heart, and bring,
as housegifts, new ones. You hear

yourselves in them,
self after self. Your solitudes
utter their runes, your own
voices begin to rise in your throats.

But soon you love me less.
I brought with me
too much, too many laden coffers,
the panoply of residence,

improper to a visit.
Silks and furs, my enormous wings,
my crutches, and my spare crutches,
my desire to please, and worse –

my desire to judge what is right.

I take up
so much space.
You are living on what you can find,

you don't want charity, and you can't
support lingering guests.

When I leave, I leave
alone, as I came.

Timothy Liu

⁓ BURNT OFFERINGS [1995]

Thoreau

My father and I have no place to go.
His wife will not let us in the house –
afraid of catching AIDS. She thinks
sleeping with men is more than a sin,
my father says, as we sit on the curb
in front of someone else's house.
Sixty-four years have made my father
impotent. Silver roots, faded black
dye mottling his hair make him look
almost comical, as if his shame
belonged to me. Last night we read
Thoreau in a steak house down the road
and wept: *If a man does not keep pace
with his companions, let him travel
to the music that he hears, however
measured or far away.* The orchards
are gone, his village near Shanghai
bombed by the Japanese, the groves
I have known in Almaden – apricot,
walnut, peach and plum – hacked down.

Barry Lopez

Desert Reservation

I'd heard so much good
about this place,
how the animals were cared for
in special exhibits. But

when I arrived I saw even
prairie dogs had gone crazy in
the viewing pits; Javelina had no mud to
squat in, to cool down; Otter was
exposed on every side, even in his den.
Wolf paced like a mustang,
tongue lolling and crazy-eyed,
unable to see anyone who looked like
he did–only Deer, dozing opposite in
a chainlink pen.

Signs explain
the animals are good because
they kill animals who like oats
or corn too much.

Skunk has sprayed himself out,
with people rapping on his glass
box. Badger's gone to sleep
under a red light and children ask
if he's dead in there (dreaming of dead
silence). And
Cougar stares like a clubbed fish
into one steel corner all morning, figuring.

Only Coyote doesn't seem to care, asleep under a
creosote bush, waiting it out.

Even the birds are walled up here,
held steady in chicken-wire cages for
the staring, for souvenir photos.
And this, on the bars for Eagle:

> *The bald eagle was*
> *taken as a fledgling*
> *from a nest in New*
> *Mexico by an*
> *Indian. He planned on*
> *pulling feathers for cer-*
> *emonial headdresses*
> *every year. The*
> *federal government seized*
> *the bird and turned*
> *it over to the*
> *Desert Reserve*
> *for safekeeping.*

Bear walks in his own
pee, smells concrete
and his own shit all day long.
He wipes his nose on the wall,
trying to kill it.

At night when management is gone,
only the night watch left,
the animals begin keening: now
voices of Wood Duck and
Turtle, of Kit Fox and everyone else,
Bear too, lift up like the bellowing
of stars and kick the walls.

14 miles away, in Tucson, are movie houses,
cold beers and roads out of town,
but they say animals know how to pass the time
well enough. And after a few beers
they'd be just like Indians–
get drunk, fall down and spoil it all.

Frank R. Maloney

⌒ HOW TO EAT A SLUG [1976]

Grandmothers in Green and Orange

1.

The mick whore, Grandma Maloney,
Would tack from dive to sinking dive
Promoting a drink, a barkeep's extra fin,
Turning a trick with a Nob Hill john
Who shook like a virgin
Before that rusting iron woman.

My father used to run a sweating dream:
That shanty Irish slut ripping his throat open,
Stabbing, slicing until the bedroom
Walls were oiled with his blood.

No one seems to know how many bastards
She left at the Christian Brothers'
Orphanage close by the Barbary Coast.
Dad was thirty when the last was whelped.
The scars and welts of charity
Were a bond among them, like the tattoos
Of ss officers & Auschwitz Jews.

2.

An honest Ulsterwoman, granny
Built her homestead on a knoll
Outside the Rosebud Reservation.
She talked with Dakotas, veterans
of the Little Big Horn.
They gave her hatchets
And calumets cut with prairie
Flowers, antelopes & stick

Men like arrows.
Warriors begging corn
Remembered George Armstrong Custer
Dying, alone, still vain for his hair.

In the first spring each year
The Rosebud bloomed, flooded
The thawing valley below her mound,
Filled with wild roses, refugee
Coyotes, social rattlers,
Ferrets, and one fastidious turtle.

Years later she would watch each night
As Klansmen burnt the Boise hills.

Thomas McGrath

⌒ PASSAGES TOWARD THE DARK [1982]

Ordonnance

During a war the poets turn to war
In praise of the merit of the death of the ball-turret gunner.
It is well arranged: each in his best manner
One bleeds, one blots – as they say, it has happened before.

After a war, who has news for the poet?
If sunrise is Easter, noon is his winey tree.
Evening arrives like a postcard from his true country
And the seasons shine and sing. Each has its note

In the song of the man in his room in his house in his head remembering
The ancient airs. It is good. But is it good
That he should rise once to his song on the fumes of blood
As a ghost to his meat? Should rise so, once, in anger

And then no more? Now the footsteps ring on the stone –
The Lost Man of the century is coming home from his work.
"They are fighting, fighting" – Oh, yes. But somewhere else. In the dark.
The poet reads by firelight as the nations burn.

⌒ LETTER TO AN IMAGINARY FRIEND [1997]

from Part One

I.

– "From here it is necessary to ship all bodies east."
I am in Los Angeles, at 2714 Marsh Street,
Writing, rolling east with the earth, drifting toward Scorpio,
                                        thinking,
Hoping toward laughter and indifference.

"They came through the passes,
            they crossed the dark mountains in a month of snow,
Finding the plain, the bitter water,
                       the iron rivers of the black North.
Horsemen,
Hunters of the hornless deer in the high plateaus of that country,
They traveled the cold year, died in the stone desert."

Aye, long ago. A long journey ago,
Most of it lost in the dark, in a ruck of tourists,
In the night of the compass, companioned by tame wolves, plagued
By theories, flies, visions, by the anthropophagi…

I do not know what end that journey was toward.
– But I am its end. I am where I have been and where
I am going. The journeying destination – at least that…
But far from the laughter.
                        So. Writing:

"The Melt of the pig pointed to early spring.
The tossed bones augured an easy crossing.
North, said the mossy fur of the high pines.
West, said the colored stone at the sulphur pool."

   II.

– And at the age of five ran away from home.
(I have never been back. Never left.) I was going perhaps
Toward the woods, toward a sound of water – called by what bird?
Leaving the ark-tight farm in its blue and mortgaged weather
To sail the want-all seas of my five dead summers
Past the dark ammonia-and-horse-piss smelling barn
And the barnyard dust, adrift in the turkey wind
Or pocked with the guinea-print and staggering script
Of the drunken-sailor ducks, a secret language; leaving
Also my skippering Irish father, land-locked Sinbad,
With his head in a song-bag and his feet stuck solid
On the quack grass-roofed and rusting poop-deck of the north forty,
In the alien corn: the feathery, bearded, and all-fathering wheat.

Leaving my mother, too, with her kindness and cookies.
The whispering, ginghamy, prayers – impossible pigeons –

Whickering into the camphor-and-cookie-crumb dark toward
God in the clothes closet.
                              Damp comforts.
                                              Tears
Harder than nails.
A mint of loving laughter.

How could I leave them?
I took them with me, though I went alone
Into the Christmas dark of the woods and down
The whistling slope of the coulee, past the Indian graves
Alive and flickering with the gopher light.

  III.

– Dry runs and practice journeys through the earthquake weather
Of the interior summer…
                                        the singing services
And ceremony cheerful as a harness bell.
– Bright flags and fictions of those hyacinthine hours
Stain and sustain me past the hell of this mumming time
Toward the high wake I would hold:
                                        No ghost, but O ill and older
Than other autumns when I ran the calico lanes
Past sleepy summer, gone, and the late west light
Downfallen. Lost. Autumn of distant voices, half heard,
Calling.
                              Rain. Gunfire. Crows. Mist, far, woods.
Farther than winter birds in the most gaunt tree
Snapped in the frost, I was; or went. Was free, and haunted
By the reeling plunge of the high hawk down – down! O down
Where the curving rabbit lunged and was slapped with a sharp and killing
Heel.
There, in the still post-solstice dark, among
Rococo snow, the harp-shaped drifts and the ghost-marked trees of the season
I went all ways…
– Spring came; the first cold rainstorms, dropping
Their electric hardware in the bright-work of the snow.
Then, the leather seasons by, and my bundling times,
My eye sustained the cow-bird and the crow,
Their feather terms…

Then horny Summer come…
– And Autumn growing
In the west steep wrestling light and the rain-wrung rheumy wind in the rag-
headed woods.

*

Way-stations on the underground journey; the boy running, running…
– Search for Lough Derg, or the holy waters of the Cheyenne,
Or the calf-deep Maple. Running away
I had the pleasure of their company…

IV.

Took them? They came –
Past the Horn, Cape Wrath, Oxford and Fifth and Main
Laughing and mourning, snug in the two-seater buggy,
Jouncing and bouncing on the gumbo roads
Or slogging loblolly in the bottom lands –
My seven-tongued family.
How could I escape? Strapped on the truckle bars
Of the bucking red-ball freights or riding the blinds cold
Or sick and sea-sawed on the seven seas
Or in metal and altitude, drilling the high blue
I fled.
I heard them laughing at the oarsmen's bench.
Conched in cowcatchers, they rambled at my side.
The seat of the buggy was wider than Texas
And slung to the axles were my rowdy cousins;
Riding the whippletrees: aunts, uncles, brothers,
Second cousins, great aunts, friends and neighbors
All holus-bolus, piss-proud, all sugar-and-shit
A goddamned gallimaufry of ancestors.
The high passes?
Hunter of the hornless deer?

V.

A flickering of gopher light. The Indian graves…
And then the river.
Companioned and alone,

Five, ten, or twenty, I followed the coulee hills
Into the dreaming green of the river shade,
The fish-stinking cow-dunged dark of the cattle-crossing,
The fox-barking, timber-wolf country, where...
The cicada was sawing down the afternoon:
Upstream a beaver was spanking Nature:
The cows were wilder:
Horses carniverous.

The kitty-corner river cut through the buggy
Through Dachau and Thaelmann
Rolfe in Spain
Through the placid, woodchuck-coughing afternoon
Drifting
Past Greenwich, Baton Rouge, Sheldon, Rome
And past Red Hook and Mobile where the rivers mourn
Old Thames, Missouri, Rio Hondo, Now
In far Los Angeles I hear
The Flying Dutchman in the dry river
Mourning. Mourning.
Ancestral night....

Passages of the dark; streets with no known turning
Beyond the sleepy midnight and the metaphysical summer
Leading here. Here. Here, queerly here.
To the east-slant light of the underground moon, and the rusty garden
Empty.
                              Bounded by ghosts.
                                        Empty except for footnotes
Of journeying far friends near.

                                        Enter now,
O bird on the green branch of the dying tree, singing
Sing me toward home:
Toward the deep past and inalienable loss:
Toward the gone stranger carrying my name
In the possible future
                              – enter now:
Purlieus and stamping grounds of hungering people
O enter

"They died in the stone desert
They crossed the dark mountain in the month of snow.
Finding the plain, the bitter water, the iron rivers of the black North."
Horns on the freeway. Footsteps of strangers,
Angelinos: visitations in the metropolitan night.

"Hunters of the hornless deer."

Ancestral baggage....

⁓ LETTER TO AN IMAGINARY FRIEND, PARTS THREE & FOUR [1985]

from Part Three

2.

And we, of the damned poor, trot our frost-furred horses
Into the barn where beyond the glinting lantern, a blessed
And a steamy animal sleep is clotting into a night
Dreamless, perhaps, or, if blurred by dreams, it is green as summer
And the hay that burns there – a cattle-barn night, star lighted
By rays from the deadwhite nailheads shining in their rime-laced albs.

The yard is corralling the darkness now, but Orient offers
A ghost-pale waning moon host-thin in the wan and failing
Light:
The sun that brief December day now gone
Toward topaz distances . . . of mineral afternoons
Beyond the Bad Lands . . .
                         toward Montana . . .
                                       the shandy westernesses . . .

And we three (who are now but one in the changed and changing
Dark of my personal fading and falling world) we three
Hand in hand and hand in heart sail to the house –
My father has lent me the light so we can go hand in hand,
Himself between us, the lantern brighter than any moon!

Indoors, my mother bends over the stove, her face rosy
In the crackling woodfire that winks and spits from an open lid.
And we are *all* there, then, as we were, once,
On the planet of sadness in a happy time. (We did not, then,
Miss you, Tomasito, an unsuffered age away
Waiting for all my errors to make me one time right.)

And so I will name them here for the last time, who were once
Upon the earth in a time greener than this:
My next brother Jim, then Joe, then my only sister, Kathleen,
Then Martin, then Jack, the baby.
                                        Now Jim and Jack have gone
Into the dark with my mother and father. But then –
                                                    Oh, then!
How bright their faces shone that lamplit Christmas Eve!
And our mother, her whole being a lamp in all times and weather . . .
And our father, the dear flesh-gantry that lifted us all from the dark . . .

    [In the transfiguring light, from the kitchen wall, a Christ
    Opens his chest like an album to show us his pierced heart
    As he peers from a church calendar almost empty of days.
    Now: say, then, who among you might not open your flesh
    On an album of loss and pain – icons of those you have loved
    Gone on without you: forever farther than Montana or sundown?
    No Christ ever suffered pain longer or stronger than this . . . 200]

So let me keep them now – and forever – fixed in that lost
Light
        as I take the lantern and go down the stairs to the cellar
In search of the Christmas apples cold in their brimming bin.
There, as deep in the hull of a ship, the silence collects
Till I hear through the dead-calm new-come night the far bells: . . .

A Coal Fire in Winter

Something old and tyrannical burning there.
(Not like a wood fire which is only
The end of a summer, or a life)
But something of darkness: heat
From the time before there was fire.
And I have come here
To warm that blackness into forms of light,
To set free a captive prince
From the sunken kingdom of the father coal.

A warming company of the cold-blooded –
These carbon serpents of bituminous gardens,
These inflammable tunnels of dead song from the black pit,
This sparkling end of the great beasts, these blazing
Stone flowers diamond fire incandescent fruit.
And out of all that death, now,
At midnight, my love and I are riding
Down the old high roads of inexhaustible light.

Three Poems

POEM

When I carry my little son in the cold
I begin to turn into a hollow tree:
I want to carry him more deeply,
Inside the warmth of my heart.

*

POEM

My little son, laughing, singing ...
Why these tears
trembling at my eyes?

    *

CELEBRATION

How wonderful, Tomasito!
All of us here!
Together ...
A little while
On the road through ...

Nuclear Winter

After the first terror
        people
Were more helpful to each other –
As in a blizzard
Much comradeliness, help, even
            laughter:
The pride of getting through tough times.

Even, months later,
When snow fell in June,
We felt a kind of pride in
                    our
"Unusual weather"
And joked about wild geese
Migrating south,
Quacking over the 4th of July presidential honkings.
It was, people said,
The way it had been in the Old Days ...

Until the hunger of the next year.

Then we came to our senses
And began to kill each other.

The Return

The trees are never the same
                              twice
                                        the animals
                                                    the birds or
The little river lying on its back in the sun or the sun or
The varying moon changing over the changing hills
Constant.
            It is this, still, that most I love about them.

I enter by dark or day:
                          that green noise, dying
Alive and living its death, that inhuman circular singing,
May call me stranger . . .
                              Or the little doors of the bark open
And I enter that other home outside the tent of my skin . . .

On such days, on such midnights, I have gone, I will go,
Past the human, past the animal, past the bird,
To the old mothers who stand with their feet in the loamy dark
And their green and gold praises playing into the sun . . .

For a little while, only. (It is a long way back.)
But at last, and if but for a moment, I have almost entered the stone.
Then fear and love call. I am cast out. Alien,
On the bridge of fur and of feather I go back to the world I have known.

⁓ DEATH SONG [1991]

Probable Cause

In the house of the man with no hands
Why are there so many filthy
Dishes:
Teacups coffee cups wine
glasses plates left over
pieces of stale bread?

Because so many loving
and delightfully thoughtless people
Come to visit here.

On the Head of a Pin

Curled like a foetus,
The drunk
Sleeps in the narrow doorway...
Enough room, I suppose,
For all the saints and buddhas....

Reading by Mechanic Light

In the early evening
The dark comes in like a heavy tide ...
The blackness empty of god –
Thank god – that dismal bed
We used to smother in.

And now the full moon
Godless – no witches' moon –
Pitches over the houses like an empty ship:
Darkening the stars in the heavens' empty
Spider web.

The moon like a white bone . . .
Now not even a witch –
Ditched into darkness, bald as a skull.
How does it pull from pole to pole,
The careless sea?

But it has the sea in thrall:
Leashed like a small dog.
And so the tides must thole
In durance vile – as we
Endure our bankruptcy –

Now neither goddess or witch –
And precious little light
To read on a page of stars
What once we dreamed was ours:
Before the light went out.

Tim McNulty

Bodhidharma Crossing the Graywolf River on a Ry-Krisp

HOMAGE TO CHUCK EASTON

As the great bhikshu descends into the West
He is met by a pilgrim who is choking
Under 90 lbs. of expensive lightweight backpacking gear.
Pilgrim clutches a small tree on a cliffside
And the how delicious berry briars
Scribble over his chest.
He is also a great bhikshu.
But Bodhidharma is curious about this prick rancher
In the valley who claims to have cleaned out
All the wolves from the Graywolf.
Bodhidharma looks like a wolf.

This is the night everyone hoped would never come.
This is why the whales moved back to the sea.
A Winnebago howls mournfully at the moon
While the last hunter slogs through the mud
Of the logged-off stumpfields of his mind.
The moon eclipses herself in disgust.
Seasons become confused.

Bodhidharma stops by a rock to enjoy the view.
Sometimes the clouds
From the pulpmill stacks drift north,
Sometimes south, like Bashō's clouds,
Only civilized.

W. S. Merwin

⌒ THE SECOND FOUR BOOKS [1993]

For a Coming Extinction

Gray whale
Now that we are sending you to The End
That great god
Tell him
That we who follow you invented forgiveness
And forgive nothing

I write as though you could understand
And I could say it
One must always pretend something
Among the dying
When you have left the seas nodding on their stalks
Empty of you
Tell him that we were made
On another day

The bewilderment will diminish like an echo
Winding along your inner mountains
Unheard by us
And find its way out
Leaving behind it the future
Dead
And ours

When you will not see again
The whale calves trying the light
Consider what you will find in the black garden
And its court
The sea cows the Great Auks the gorillas
The irreplaceable hosts ranged countless
And foreordaining as stars
Our sacrifices

Join your word to theirs
Tell him
That it is we who are important

Avoiding News by the River

As the stars hide in the light before daybreak
Reed warblers hunt along the narrow stream
Trout rise to their shadows
Milky light flows through the branches
Fills with blood
Men will be waking

In an hour it will be summer
I dreamed that the heavens were eating the earth
Waking it is not so
Not the heavens
I am not ashamed of the wren's murders
Nor the badger's dinners
On which all worldly good depends
If I were not human I would not be ashamed of anything

The Gardens of Zuñi

The one-armed explorer
could touch only half of the country
In the virgin half
the house fires give no more heat
than the stars
it has been so these many years
and there is no bleeding

He is long dead with his five fingers
and the sum of their touching
and the memory
of the other hand
his scout

that sent back no message
from where it had reached
with no lines in its palm
while he balanced
balanced
and groped on
for the virgin land

and found where it had been

Second Psalm: The Signals

When the ox-horn sounds in the buried hills
    of Iceland
    I am alone
    my shadow runs back into me to hide
    and there is not room for both of us
    and the dread
when the ox-horn sounds on the blue stairs
    where the echoes are my mother's name
    I am alone
    as milk spilled in a street
    white instrument
    white hand
    white music
when the ox-horn is raised like a feather in one
    of several rivers
    not all of which I have come to
    and the note starts toward the sea
    I am alone
    as the optic nerve of the blind
    though in front of me it is written
    This is the end of the past
    Be happy
when the ox-horn sounds from its tassels of blood
    I always seem to be opening
    a book an envelope the top of a well
    none of them mine
    a tray of gloves has been set down

beside my hands
I am alone
as the hour of the stopped clock
when the ox-horn is struck by its brother
    and the low grieving denial
    gropes forth again with its black hands
    I am alone
    as one stone left to pray in the desert
    after god had unmade himself
    I am
    I still am
when the ox-horn sounds over the dead oxen
    the guns grow light in hands
    I the fearer
    try to destroy me the fearing
    I am alone
    as a bow that has lost its nerve
    my death sinks into me to hide
    as water into stones
    before a great cold
when the ox-horn is raised in silence
    someone's breath is moving over my face
    like the flight of a fly
    but I am in this world
    without you
    I am alone as the sadness surrounding
    what has long ministered to our convenience
    alone as the note of the horn
    as the human voice
    saddest of instruments
    as a white grain of sand falling in a still sea
    alone as the figure she unwove each night alone

    alone
    as I will be

An Encampment at Morning

A migrant tribe of spiders
spread tents at dusk in the rye stubble
come day I see the color
of the planet under their white-beaded tents
where the spiders are bent
by shade fires in damp September
to their live instruments
and I see the color of the planet
when their tents go from above it
as I come that way in a breath of cloud
learning my steps
among the tents rising invisibly like the shapes of snowflakes
we are words on a journey
not the inscriptions of settled people

Berryman

I will tell you what he told me
in the years just after the war
as we then called
the second world war

don't lose your arrogance yet he said
you can do that when you're older
lose it too soon and you may
merely replace it with vanity

just one time he suggested
changing the usual order
of the same words in a line of verse
why point out a thing twice

he suggested I pray to the Muse
get down on my knees and pray

right there in the corner and he
said he meant it literally

it was in the days before the beard
and the drink but he was deep
in tides of his own through which he sailed
chin sideways and head tilted like a tacking sloop

he was far older than the dates allowed for
much older than I was he was in his thirties
he snapped down his nose with an accent
I think he had affected in England

as for publishing he advised me
to paper my wall with rejection slips
his lips and the bones of his long fingers trembled
with the vehemence of his view about poetry

he said the great presence
that permitted everything and transmuted it
in poetry was passion
passion was genius and he praised movement and invention

I had hardly begun to read
I asked how can you ever be sure
that what you write is really
any good at all and he said you can't

you can't you can never be sure
you die without knowing
whether anything you wrote was any good
if you have to be sure don't write

Jane Miller

~ AMERICAN ODALISQUE [1987]

Topos

At the documentary level, a voice on tape
survives an instant, chatting about
politics, money and love, then is extinct.
The language is local and commercial.
It fractures a moment. On the screen,
meanwhile, on a darkened nightclub stage,
a star moves. One is not oneself
on stage, one enters an autistic drift
with music. For example, I hear storks
in the background, a whistle, an electronic
synthesizer, a metallic bird. It isn't spring,
but the organist plants seeds. Then I'm part
of the audience.

If I call and the phone monitor is on
they will hear me ask for her
and be able to talk about me while I'm talking.
Behind them is a South American
wood flute serenade. Sounds like wind
through empty Pepsi bottles. Heads swaying,
hands snapping. It's a devotional exercise
and the carnations and tulips in their living
room, couched like talk show guests, show them
watching TV, tourists at home. I call,
finally feeling at home in the motel,
listening to music, wanting nothing of my own,

everything to belong to my mate and my mate to me.

American Odalisque

Schwinn rests in back seat
of my blue convertible;
leaving, I'm sorry.

*

Snails sprawl fine sad, dawn
spills like waste into the sea.
I don't care either.

*

Mobil Station next
rest stop, where I phone my love.
Busy; no answer.

*

Coked & dancing, I
think of Cape Cod now, your voice.
Shivering barstool.

*

I'm safe now in town.
I sleep late with my new love.
Remember? Say yes.

*

Cool, professional,
like a river is a slave
for sun, I seek love.

*

Pepsi & money
flow easy; I need you here
while I am just past young.

                   *

I stall on the bridge,
press my emergency light.
Berkeley, a lifetime.

                   *

Midnight. Heaven is
bathing, the window open.
Just a kiss away.

                   *

Aren't they always
mistaken for images,
your Invisibles?

                   *

A coyote, bats,
they put me in no mood here,
I can't touch myself.

                   *

And think of the moon
who is my family since
I have no children.

                   *

Are fish unconscious
and mute? Last night I ate one
in lime sauce. Years pass.

                   *

My car, your shadows.
Roadrunner skids to the door.
My friends are scattered.

*

What will the new art
be made of? Dusk, a snowfall,
same cold human feet.

*

Easter Sunday sun.
Stewardesses picketing
United parade.

⌣ AUGUST ZERO [1993]

Poetry

Invited onto the grounds of the god,
who decides what words mean,
we are amazed at the world
perfect at last. Gold fish, gold finches, gold watches,
trash blasted into crystal, all
twilights supporting one final sunset
with slender fingers of consolation.
A little reality goes a long way,
far off in the distance the weak sea
beaches its blue whales, the small sky
melds the stars into one
serious fire, burning eternally
out of control, our earth.
But here we are visiting
the plutonium factory dazzling
to the eye, the one good one remaining
to us in our wisdom. We have concluded
that automatic, volcanic sunrises and sunsets
where light trips on the same cardboard vine

are blinding, and we would rather fail
painfully slowly than survive a copy
of the world perfect at last. Yet we are
impressed by the real thing, which we walk
like dew upon flesh, suddenly lubricated and translucent
beyond our dreamiest desires, hard-pressed
to object. Consoled that there is so little
difference between the terrible and the real,
we admire the powerful appleseeds bobbing
in the dewy pools, we cannot help
but enjoy their greeny spring, and it is only by resting
on the miraculous grass, wildly uniform, mildly serene,
that we sense
with our secret selves, the little bit we left behind and
remember, that we are out of our element, that we are
being made into words even as we speak.

MEMORY AT THESE SPEEDS: NEW AND SELECTED POEMS [1996]

Which Religion Vouchsafes

At the end of emotion & description there is a village
there are marriages & funerals there is a trailer
someone without capital works away
half-hidden in the immense open range
a wedding Ford streams crepe paper
flashes & toasts lift the parish hall
nearby a stream waters small fields of beans
onlookers in dressclothes waltz the school gym
self-conscious fabulation on fabulation
one-story adobes with two or three rooms
pitched tin that shines in the sun
long front porches
when they leave their houses they keep an eye out
for stray hens or for dead cedar for post
what I have seen almost everywhere corresponds to the earlier
& true time one has no right to claim
the consequence of this is the only possible one
it is possible that another person is born

of tenderness & fantasy
institutions which daily battle for dominance
at a cattle roundup and rodeo
the value of which is not to be looked into
at the other end of the street screams a slaughterhouse
no one ought to breathe a word of it
free from images & determined solely
by structure the thin white bark of a sycamore
tenders assignations as befitting the time and circumstance
scattered throughout ranch country
the amorous spaces must be seen
as dreams bound & consumed
when they can't sleep they go out bareheaded
for a cool drink
as apparitions who know carnal love

O Pioneers!

Massive rock head but the guy's eyes dart
like cars racing the water's edge
right and left the gleaming corneas
of the wolf just as you remember Mussolini
smiling counting off twenty shots
into a policeman's kiosk on Via del Whatever
and the girl looks to be
eighteen is twelve none of this made up
all of it twenty minutes ago
the shooting the embrace the robbery the divorce
the monument to them and the aerial ballet that
leveled them the criminal and girl
iconographically strung across a bridge because there isn't land
to explain their unhappiness
as the water underneath has no explanation
cut short damn it
love is a steep fall from your perspective
aimless harmless but from mine grim and grim
the wide spaces the swashbuckling energy
toothless now and tasteless that cowboy that showgirl

America's triumvirate him and her and
me/you inheritors of the latter day
when your amalgam of discrete enthusiasm
settles into sexual fantasy and stereotype
indeed settles voluntarily
what then on Via del Whatever and on Saint
Street it's not a design it's a feeling
that you've gone off on a long trip
with an incision in your rock head
and a dart through one eye though you haven't known
her for long not that that matters in love
god turned to follow your small figure
with encouragement by the light of the moon
to live off each truth
a marriage a crown and a wallet
each tall grass a cry and starlight a rock
with a brother and a mother like yours
our voluptuous words hang volcanically
seven balconies face the sun in our tragedy
forty-three daffodils preen in the hills
we don't see dying

O.V. de L. Milosz

⌒ FOURTEEN POEMS [1983]

La Berline arrêtée dans la nuit

Waiting for the keys
– He is probably looking for them
Among the clothes
Of Thecla, dead for thirty years –
Listen, Madam, listen to the old deaf muttering
Of the nocturnal avenue ...
So little and so weak, two times enveloped in my cloak,
I will carry you through the briars, and nettles, across the ruins
    up to the high black gate
Of the chateau.
So it was that a grandfather, long ago, returned
From Vercelli with a dead woman.
What a mute, suspicious, black house
For my child!
You know it already, Madam, it is a sad story.
They sleep, scattered in distant countries.
For a hundred years
Their place waits for them,
In the heart of the hill.
With me their race is extinct.
O Lady of the ruins!
We are going to see the beautiful room of childhood: there,
The supernatural depth of silence
Is the voice of the dim portraits.

Curled upon my couch at night,
I heard, like in hollow armor,
Like the thaw dripping in the wall,
the beating of their hearts.
What a savage country for my timid child!
The lantern goes out, the moon is veiled.
The barn owl calls to his girls in the thicket.
While we wait for the keys,

Sleep a little, Madam, sleep, my poor child, sleep
All pale, your head on my shoulder.
You will see how the anxious forest
Is beautiful in the insomnias of June, dressed
In flowers, o my child, like the chosen daughter
Of the Midsummer Night Queen.
Wrap yourself in my traveling cloak:
The huge autumn snowflakes melt on your face;
And you are sleepy.
(In the rays of the lantern she turns, turns in the wind
As in my childhood dreams
The old woman – you understand, – the old woman.)
No, Madam, I hear nothing.
He is very aged,
His head is deranged.
I guess he went for a drink.

So black a house for my timid child!
Deep, deep, in the Lithuanian countryside.
No, Madam, I hear nothing.
House black, black,
Rusty locks,
Dead vines,
Bolted doors,
Closed shutters,
Leaves on leaves for a hundred years in the parkways.
All the servants are dead.
Me, I have lost my memory.
So black a house for a trusting child!
I can remember only the orangerie
Of my great great grandfather, the theater:
Baby owls used to eat from my hand there.
The moon looking through the jasmine.
That was long ago.
I hear a step at the bottom of the parkway.
A shadow. Here is Witold with the keys.

Translated from the French by Kenneth Rexroth

James Masao Mitsui

⌢ JOURNAL OF THE SUN [1974]

Nisei: Second Generation Japanese-American

They grow over the Yangtze, the plum rains
grow over water that drops
gently to the wideness of the East China Sea.
Farmers in Kyushu are caught by the floating clouds,
squinting to see who it is
standing there on the dirt bank, the mud
in the soft rain, soft as the leading edge of a cloud.

I write this on a day that has been twisted away
from doubt. Happy to be here
still I have a place on that gray continent,
far home of my grandfathers
those figures I never saw through the haze
of mountains except in picture. Photographs
yellow and brown as old newsprint,
smudges of thought, of fingers and skin.
Time to realize the importance of rain.
Rain on the ground,
and rain still falling.

Miyoshi Toyoichiro

⌒ LIKE UNDERGROUND WATER [1995]

Shadow 1

The sound of shoes going down to the grave in the dark
tremulously, endlessly.
Lonely dialogue from downstairs, like prayer, like repentance.
It suddenly ceases.
I put on the light. So that the dark cannot steal me away,
I only let the light spread out around me
and begin to smoke, hoping for a little pleasure at least.
An unshaven, hollow-cheeked, sorrowful, yet familiar face
stares at me from behind the cold darkness beyond.
A lonely lord –
my small, round territory expands with the glow!
I put out the light and I fall.
I lose myself, and in the dark, as if groping for black death,
I touch someone's face.

Translated from the Japanese by Naoshi Koriyama and Edward Lueders

Robin Morgan

~ DEATH BENEFITS [1981]

Battery

The fist meets the face as the stone meets water.
I want to understand the stone's parabola
and where the ripples disappear,
to make the connections, to trace
the withholding of love as the ultimate violence.

Battery: a word with seven letters, seven definitions:

1) Any unit, apparatus, or grouping
in which a series or set of parts or components
is assembled to serve a common end.
2) *Electrical*. One or more primary or secondary cells
operating together as a single source of direct current.
3) *Military*. A tactical artillery unit.
4) *A Game position*. In baseball, the pitcher
and catcher together.
5) *Law*. The illegal beating or touching of another person.
6) *Music*. The percussion instruments of an orchestra.
7) *Optics*. The group of prisms in a spectroscope.

I want to understand the connections
– between the tower where Bertha Mason Rochester
is displayed to Jane Eyre as a warning
– with this place, the city my doorstep
where I've learned to interfere between
the prostitute's scream and the pimp's knife
is to invite their unified disgust.

I want to understand the components:
– the stone's parabola, the percussion instruments,
the growth of battered children into battered wives
who beat their children,

– the beating of the fallow deer in Central Park Zoo
by unknown teenage assailants,
– the beating of these words against the poem:
to hit, slap, strike, punch, slash, stamp,
pound, maul, pummel, hammer, bludgeon, batter –
to hurt, to wound,
to flex the fist and clench the jaw and withhold love.

I want to discover the source of direct current,
to comprehend the way the primary or secondary cells
operate together as that source:
– the suburban community's defense of the fugitive Nazi
discovered to be a neighbor,
– the effect of her father's way with women
on the foreign policy of Elizabeth Tudor,
– the volunteers for a Utah firing squad,
the manner in which kwashiorkor – Red Johnny,
the Ghanaians call this slow death by starvation –
turns the hair of children a coppery color
with the texture of frayed wire.

I want to follow the refractions of the prism:
– the water's surface shuddering in anticipation
of the arching pebble,
– the oilslick mask imposed on the Pacific,
– the women of the Irish peace movement accused
of being traitors to tactical artillery units on both sides,
and replying, "We must accept that
in the next few months we will become their targets."
– The battering of dolphins against tuna nets,
– the way celosia, a flower commonly known
as cockscomb, is bulbous, unpetaled, and a dark velvet red –
and always reminds me of a hemorrhaging brain.

The danger in making the connections
is to lose the focus,
and this is not a poem about official torture
in Iran or Chile or China, or a poem about
a bald eagle flailing its wings as it dies,
shot down over Long Island.

This is a poem called "Battery" about a specific woman
who is twelve-going-on-seventy-three and who
exists in any unit, grouping, class, to serve a common end.
A woman who is black and white and bruised all over
the world, and has no other place to go
– while the Rolling Stones demand shelter
– and some cops say it's her own fault for living with him
– and some feminists say it's her own fault for living with him,
and she hides her dark red velvet wounds
from pride, the pride of the victim,
the pride of the victim at not
being the perpetrator,
the pride of the victim at not knowing how
to withhold love.

The danger of fixing on the focus
is to lose the connections, and this is a poem
about the pitcher and the catcher *together*:
– the battery of Alice Toklas, conversing cookbooks
with the other wives while Gertrude Stein shared her cigars
and her ideas with the men,
– the sullen efficiency of Grace Poole,
– the percussion of my palm striking my husband's face
in fury when he won't learn how to fight back, how to outgrow
having been a battered child, his mother's battered wince
rippling from his eyes, his father's laborer's fingers
flexing my fist, the pitcher and the catcher together
teaching me how to withhold love;
the contempt of the perpetrator for the pride of the victim.
The collaboration, the responsibility, the intimate
violence, the fantasy, the psychic battery, the lies,
the beating of the heart.

To fear, to dread, to cower, cringe, flinch,
shudder, to skulk, to shuffle.

Wing-beat, heart-beat,
the fist meets the face as the stone displaces water,
as the elbow is dislocated from the socket
and the connections shatter from the focus;

– the knifeblade glimmers in the streetlight;
– it could be a drifting eagle feather
or cigar smoke rising
graceful as a doe who leaps in pain,
rising livid as a welt, livid as a consciousness
of my own hand falling to dispense
the bar of soap, the executioner's axe, the tuna nets,
the rifle, and at last the flint
for Bertha Mason Rochester to strike,
to spark the single source of direct current,
to orchestrate the common end emprismed
in the violent ripples of withheld love.

Batter my heart, seven-petaled word, for you
as yet but flower inside my brain;
that I may understand the stone's parabola,
make the connections, remember the focus,
comprehend the definitions,
and withhold nothing.

Pablo Neruda

~ STILL ANOTHER DAY [1983]

VI.

Pardon me, if when I want
to tell the story of my life
it's the land I talk about.
This is the land.
It grows in your blood
and you grow.
If it dies in your blood
you die out.

Translated from the Spanish by William O'Daly

XIII.

Men grow with all that grows
and Pedro rises with his river,
with the tree that climbs without words,
for this my word grows
and grows:
it comes from that silence with roots,
from the days of wheat,
from those untransferable germs,
from the vast water,
from the closed sun without its consent,
from the horses sweating in the rain.

Translated from the Spanish by William O'Daly

XXVII.

Still, I am here.
We all are.
The good citizens, the bloodthirsty,
the hatmakers who passed through life
measuring my head and your head,
the beltmakers
who stuck to each waist,
to each breast of the world.
We're going to line up elbow to elbow
with the anchorites,
the young with the indigestion of guerrillas,
with the traditionalists who were bewildered
because nobody wanted to eat shit.
But moreover,
integrity of the new day,
youth of the dew,
morning of the world,
whatever else grows despite
the bitter weather:
we need pure order.

Translated from the Spanish by William O'Daly

~ THE SEPARATE ROSE [1985]

Introduction: My Themes

To Easter Island and the presences
I set out, fed up with doorways and streets,
to search for something I never lost there.
The month of January, so dry,
it resembles a spike of wheat:
its golden light hangs from Chile
until the sea washes it away

and I leave only to come back again.

Statues that night raised
and threshed in a closed circle
so the ocean alone would see them.

(I traveled there to recover them, to erect them
in my house that has vanished.)

And here, surrounded by gray presences,
by whiteness of space, by blue motion,
by sea water, clouds, stone,
I begin the lives of my life again.

Translated from the Spanish by William O'Daly

~ WINTER GARDEN [1986]

Homecomings

Two homecomings sustained my life
and the daily sea, ebbing and rising:
at once I faced the light, the earth,
a certain provisional peace. The moon
was an onion, nourishing globe
of the night, the orange sun
submerged in the sea:
an arrival that
I endured and kept buried until now,
it was my will and here I shall remain:
now my homecoming is the truth.

I felt it as a blow,
like a crystal nut
shattering on a boulder
and in that way, in a thunderclap, the light flashed,
the light of the littoral, of the lost sea,
of the sea captured now and forever.

I am a man of so many homecomings
that form a cluster of betrayals,
and again, I leave on a frightening voyage
in which I travel and never arrive anywhere:
my single journey is a homecoming.

And this time among seductions
I was afraid to touch the sand, the sparkle
of this wounded and scattered sea,
but accepting of my unjust acts
my decision fell with the sound
of a glass fruit that shatters
and in this resounding blow I glimpsed life,
the earth wrapped in shadows and sparks
and the cup of the sea below my lips.

Translated from the Spanish by William O'Daly

⌇ STONES OF THE SKY [1987]

XI.

From the explosion to the iron split,
from the crevice to the road,
from the quake to the fire,
to the turning, to the river,
that heart of sky-water, heart of gold
stayed still
and each vein of jasper or sulphur
was a rush, was a wing,
was a drop of fire or of dew.

Does the rock live without moving or growing?

Does the marine agate really have lips?

I will not answer because I cannot:
so it was, the churning genesis

of glowing and growing stones
that live on, ever since, in the cold.

Translated from the Spanish by James Nolan

~ THE SEA AND THE BELLS [1988]

Every Day, Matilde

Today, I dedicate this to you: you are long
like the body of Chile, delicate
like an anise flower,
and in every branch you bear witness
to our indelible springtimes:
What day is today? Your day.
And tomorrow is yesterday, it has not passed,
the day never slipped from your hands:
you guard the sun, the earth, the violets
in your slender shadow when you sleep.
And in this way, every morning
you give me life.

Translated from the Spanish by William O'Daly

[untitled]

Forgive me if my eyes see
no more clearly than sea foam,
please forgive that my form
grows outward without license
and never stops:
monotonous is my song,
my word is a shadow bird,
fauna of stone and sea, the grief
of a winter planet, incorruptible.
Forgive me this sequence of water,

of rock, of foam, of the tide's
delirium: this is my loneliness:
salt in sudden leaps against the walls
of my secret being, in such a way
that I am a part
of winter,
of the same flat expanse that repeats
from bell to bell, in wave after wave,
and from a silence like a woman's hair,
a silence of seaweed, a sunken song.

Translated from the Spanish by William O'Daly

~ THE YELLOW HEART [1990]

The Hero

On a Santiago street
a naked man lived
for many long years, yes,
without lacing up, no, he never dressed,
but he always wore a hat.

His body clad only in hairs,
this philosophical fellow
appeared at times on the balcony
and the citizens viewed him
as a lonely nudist,
enemy of shirts,
of trousers and overcoats.

So it was, the fashions came and went,
vests withered
and certain lapels returned
certain walking sticks fell:
everything was resurrection
and burials in street clothes,
everything, except that mortal

naked, as he came into the world,
scornful as the patron gods
of athletics.

(The men and women who witnessed
the peculiar neighbor
gave details that shake me
with proof of the transformation
of the man and his physiology.)

After all that nudity,
after forty years of being naked
from head to toe,
he was covered with black scales
and long hair covered his eyes
such that he could never read again,
not even the dailies.

In this way, his thoughts remain
fixed on a point in the past,
as on some old editorial
in a defunct newspaper.

(A curious case, that fellow
who died as he was chasing
his canary on the terrace.)

Once again, this story proves
pure faith cannot withstand
the assaults of winter.

Translated from the Spanish by William O'Daly

Love Song

I love you, I love you, is my song
and here my silliness begins.

I love you, I love you my lung,

I love you, I love you my wild grapevine,
and if love is like wine:
you are my predilection
from your hands to your feet:
you are the wineglass of hereafter
and my bottle of destiny.

I love you forwards and backwards,
and I don't have the tone or timbre
to sing you my song,
my endless song.

On my violin that sings out of tune
my violin declares,
I love you, I love you my double bass,
my sweet woman, dark and clear,
my heart, my teeth,
my light and my spoon,
my salt of the dim week,
my clear windowpane moon.

Translated from the Spanish by William O'Daly

~ THE BOOK OF QUESTIONS [1991]

III.

Tell me, is the rose naked
or is that her only dress?

Why do trees conceal
the splendor of their roots?

Who hears the regrets
of the thieving automobile?

Is there anything in the world sadder
than a train standing in the rain?

XIV.

And what did the rubies say
standing before the juice of pomegranates?

Why doesn't Thursday talk itself
into coming after Friday?

Who shouted with glee
when the color blue was born?

Why does the earth grieve
when the violets appear?

XVIII.

How did the grapes come to know
the cluster's party line?

And do you know which is harder,
to let run to seed or to do the picking?

It is bad to live without a hell:
aren't we able to reconstruct it?

And to position sad Nixon
with his buttocks over the brazier?

Roasting him on low
with North American napalm?

LXXIII.

Who works harder on earth,
a human or the grain's sun?

Between the fir tree and the poppy
whom does the earth love more?

Between the orchids and the wheat
which does it favor?

Why a flower with such opulence
and wheat with its dirty gold?

Does autumn enter legally
or is it an underground season?

Translated from the Spanish by William O'Daly

Sheila Nickerson

~ SONGS OF THE PINE-WIFE [1980]

12.

A seal's cry has lain against my leg,
Newborn, to slip away in fog.

Once more I swell with birth,
My belly now a continent
Encircled by the currents of the sea.
My aura darkens into depths
Where stars could fall and hide.
I rise, an island of few trees,
Where voyagers might land
To rest along the drift
Of dark creation.

43.

At Auke Bay the whales dance,
Their flukes the drum of joy.
Sea lions bark; wind barks back.
My words can't meet the rain.
Listen now to these small sounds;
A life is passing here.
Past conversations strew the ground
And lie among the kelp,
The garden of the gulls.
Words and written letters fly with feathers
In the clouds. Finally, I say, taste:
My blood is salt, an ocean that you cross.
Your keel scrapes my shallows,
But I have rolled away.
I wait, with whales, there across the bay,
Their spouting air my radar
Clear against the migratory coast.

Bill O'Daly

The Whale in the Web

Early sun grazes
the green crystal hills.
Below the fathoms of fog burn off
in the narrow valley
winding one rivulet to the sea.

From my sleeping bag
I crawl past the woodstove
and the house you built creaks
like the ribcage
of a landlocked whale.
Still drunk with sleep
I piss off the high porch –
one yellow ribbon unfurls
down this *tierra de sangre*, blood red,
with tufts of grass, thistle, madrone,
and the ranks of conifers
guarding the dry spring.

A small herd of cows
start their climb; empty,
they wobble upstream towards their turn
on the south-sloping pasture.
On land we call *ours*
my woman reads and rubs her back
against a thick double fir
whose branches last night, raucous with birds,
cradled the white intruder moon.

At the first whiff of bear
the deer skipped out
thru the dark doors of the forest.

Dogs drove a porcupine higher up
the hills. Sand Creek lost its way,
paused and scanned the bent path of the moon, stopped,
waited for the dawn.

I let go my breath
and the whole house quivers
in the wet web of the land,
land that belongs to us,
that belongs to no one.
And the arteries of water,
the dance of our dead,
the tiny lungs of the living,
the pulse of the sea, spoken or unspoken,
billows its unbreakable threads.

Ou-yang Hsiu

~ LOVE AND TIME [1989]

The Pear Leaves Redden, Cicada's Song is Done

The pear leaves redden, the cicada's song is done.
Wind high up in the River of Heaven,
flute sounds: cold and cutting.
A chill on the mat, the water-clock dripping.
Who taught the swallows to make so light of parting?

At the edge of the grass the insects moan,
as autumn's frosts congeal.
Stale wine: awakening,
I can't remember when you left.
How much of what I really feel is left unsaid?
Night after night moon dawns
upon my pearl-embroidered screen.

Translated from the Chinese by J. P. Seaton

Mark Pawlak

~ THE BUFFALO SEQUENCE [1977]

After Burying Her Son, A Mother Speaks:

(FOR PAUL PLOUFFE 1948–1973.
DIED: "CAUSE UNKNOWN.")

what did she know,
with one son dead less than a year?
her poverty wasn't so great, *then,*
as how she felt:
there was nothing left they could take from her:
now that her other son,
– Paul's dead too!

herself that saw him off on a bus for California,
what did she know that day?
– to start over again to live? California,
she should laugh now,
but a son's death
severs the cord of his mother's living.
– to remain here, he'd said,
only more of the same trouble
he would get into.

a poor woman's poverty is never *so* great,
something always they will find to take from her.
thus what they forced on Paul's lips that would smile:
the smallest crack of cynicism,
in order that his life
all fit
into the size of that coffin!
even how his mother remembers him,
now they are trying to steal from her.
coroner,
as if you name it a crime, his birth.

what does she know,
how a woman is wise and knows things?
as the rain falls, only this:
that where joy dwells, or what passes for it,
she knows can't be got to,
not from here!
never simply
getting behind the car wheel, NO.

more rain and despairing.
what she knows is that rainwater
seeps,
according to its nature, across the windowsill:
this window that never closed proper.
this woman would shut the door to weeping
but knows it's her own;
uncontrollable weeping, this,
that comes,
two bony elbows, to the kitchen table.
her want
never owned the price of a dry season.

Ezra Pound

1.

The great learning (adult study, grinding corn in the head's mortar to fit it for use) takes root in clarifying the way wherein the intelligence increases through the process of looking straight into one's own heart and acting on the results; it is rooted in watching with affection the way people grow; it is rooted in coming to rest, being at ease in perfect equity.

2.

Know the point of rest and then have an orderly mode of procedure; having this orderly procedure one can "grasp the azure," that is, take hold of a clear concept; holding a clear concept one can be at peace (internally), being thus calm one can keep one's head in moment of danger; he who can keep his head in the presence of a tiger is qualified to come to his deed in due hour.

3.

Things have roots and branches; affairs have scopes and beginnings. To know what precedes and what follows, is nearly as good as having a head and feet.

4.

The men of old wanting to clarify and diffuse throughout the empire that light which comes from looking straight into the heart and then acting, first set up good government in their own states; wanting good government in their states they first established order in their families; wanting order in the home, they first disciplined themselves; desiring self-discipline, they rectified their own hearts; and wanting to rectify their hearts, they sought precise verbal definitions of their inarticulate thoughts (the tones given off by the heart); wishing to attain precise verbal definitions, they set to extend their knowledge to the utmost. This completion of knowledge is rooted in sorting things into organic categories.

5.

When things had been classified in organic categories, knowledge moved toward fulfillment; given the extreme knowable points, the inarticulate thoughts were defined with precision(the sun's lance coming to rest on the precise spot verbally). Having attained this precise verbal definition (*aliter*, this sincerity), they then stabilized their hearts, they disciplined themselves; having attained self-discipline, they set their own houses in order; having order in their own homes, they brought good government to their own states; and when their states were well governed, the empire was brought into equilibrium.

6.

From the Emperor, Son of Heaven, down to the common man, singly and all together, this self-discipline is the root.

7.

If the root be in confusion, nothing will be well governed. The solid cannot be swept away as trivial, nor can trash be established as solid. It just doesn't happen. "Take not cliff for morass and treacherous bramble."

Belle Randall

Be He Ezra Pound, Kennedy, or King

The martyr wears a crown
bestowed by circumstance.

The old ceremonial Lincoln
is the car in which his widow rides
remembering:

Reality, he defined as: "The force
of an old proverb, driven home."

And now, amid the gleam
of black upholstery and windshield rain,
his words return,

nailing down –
                    driving home
his body banked with flowers.

W. M. Ransom

~ FINDING TRUE NORTH [1973]

Message from Ohanapecosh Glacier

I have seen the soft light flicker,
seen the nose and fingers pressed flat,
fogging the ice at my feet, sinking.
That is no spirit.
Chants echo white in her deep eyes,
blackening visions shift hourly above her face.
She is never dry.
Put your ear to the ice:
a long, stuttering groan.
She is blue, arthritic, naked.
She hunts a lover.
Leave everything here.
Her trail is this twisting stream
that she sends, milky, to the sea.

~ WAVING ARMS AT THE BLIND [1975]

Pastime Café

The eyes in this place droop
thick puckers under the eyes
folds under necks droop
jowls and the plants in the windows
droop plants in the pictures on the walls
droop cigars in racks
bowling trophies, unmatched silver droops
this table and its cracked vinyl chairs
droop warm salads, year-old crackers
droop my tired hands droop

Eddy Arnold droops from the jukebox
I wake up away from you again
and my whole body droops.

David Ray

~ NOT FAR FROM THE RIVER: POEMS FROM THE GĀTHĀ SAPTAŚATI
[1990]

1.

Why do these prudes fear Prakrit poetry,
our music, and the blunt facts of love?
They draw back from that nectar,
yet wince as if they taste love's ashes.

3.

Jewels wherever we look –
that white crane on a motionless lotus –
like a conch on a dish made of emeralds,
polished at least for a lifetime.

4.

Rare sight, a woman lost in the trance,
making love. Beautiful – so long as her eyes
remain open, like blue of the lotus.
Then her pleasure gets ugly, too busy, intent.

5.

She likes it, the conjugal act.
But she smiles, her lotus-like face turned,
knowing he chooses this auspicious hour of dawn
neither for her nor himself, just for good luck.

Tom Rea

⁓ MAN IN A ROWBOAT [1977]

Lugs Benedict on the Coast, 1934

He dreams of saxophones and hounds
baying in mesquite. Gulls dive the murk.
Gold and evening move across the Sound.

Down in kelp, dolphin songs surround
the rocks. He calls them Lucy, they moan back
dreams of saxophones and hounds.

Sea mud licks his boots. Waves pound
dust from his lips. His hands go wet.
Gold and evening move across the Sound

like seasons. Seals come crowned
with light. They thrive in bulk
and sing like saxophones and hounds.

A chinook broke ice one night, his sister drowned
in Horse Creek. Her bones beach up
gold when evening moves across the Sound.

Years shove his eyes around.
Whales breach and blow the sea like milk.
He dreams of saxophones and hounds.
Gold and evening move across the Sound.

Kenneth Rexroth

~ THE SILVER SWAN [1976]

Poem

As the full moon rises
The swan sings
In sleep
On the lake of the mind

Asagumori

On the forest path
The leaves fall. In the withered
Grass the crickets sing
Their last songs. Through dew and dusk
I walk the paths you once walked,
My sleeves wet with memory.

David Romtvedt

Kiev, the Ukraine, Nuclear Accident

In the world we've made
a cloud approaches Wyoming,
a radioactive cloud born in fire,
a graphite fire in a nuclear power plant
gone wrong. The fire will not stop.

For three days it has been raining.
In Oregon people are advised not to drink rainwater.
And in Washington and Idaho. Here in Buffalo, Wyoming,
our town water comes from Clear Creek flowing
down out of the Bighorn Mountains
and through the center of town,
beside the Busy Bee Café,
under the bridge on Main Street.
The rain falls, the water flows.
All the water that can makes its way
to the creek out of which we drink.

I sigh and with that sigh I am a child
standing face up in a heavy rain –
southern Arizona, the dark sky, the water tumbling
from the foreign clouds and sluicing along
a gutterless street. My eyes are closed
so I feel the drops pelt my eyelids.
My mouth is open as wide as I can open it,
tongue hanging out. The rain pounds
on my tongue but does not hurt.

I love this feeling and, as my mouth fills,
I swallow – cool water on what, thirty minutes before,
was another hot day. I let my arms rise
away from my sides and I begin to turn,

to spin in place like the blades of a propeller,
or those seeds with wings that come down from the trees
like eggbeaters upside down, or a ballet dancer
I have never seen. The water flies off
the ends of my fingers as it continues
to strike my tongue. Around and around
until I am so dizzy I fall and lie on my back,
eyes still closed, mouth still open. My mother
comes out in the yard to watch the rain.
She speaks to me and I look at her.
She smiles. The she lies down next to me.
Side by side on our backs we both close our eyes,
open our mouths and drink the rain
that goes on falling.

Richard Shelton

Promises

When America closes for the night
and the last ferryboat leaves Port Townsend,
those of us left behind
cannot remember where it is going.

Low tide hesitates, gathers its strength
and begins to return, bringing driftwood,
seaweed torn up by the roots
and a little light to help us
find our way home. If we were drunker
or younger, we think we might sprawl here
on the beach all night, listening
to the sea's absolute authority
and to foghorns calling each other
like lost and lovesick whales.

But we are no longer boys
who can sleep where we fall and wake
to begin a new journey. We have made
many promises and kept some.
We have wives who are not waiting up
for us but whose eyes will open
no matter how quietly we open the door,
and close again when we close it,
having seen in that moment everything,
understood everything, and forgiven nothing.

Maurya Simon

⌒ THE ENCHANTED ROOM [1986]

Blue Movies

His fingers are caterpillars balanced
on the bough of her body.
Her legs snake around his trunk,
her arms entwine over his broad back.

The moans of the lovers float
above the heads of the Latino ushers,
past the ticket office where ID is required,
to the old men who are waiting in line
outside the theater in the black drizzle.
Some hold umbrellas as if they were candles,
other collect their breath in their hands.
One man studies a small red mole
protruding from the ticket taker's lip.

The line moves forward.
Thank you, they say, as they move out
of one darkness into another.

⌒ DAYS OF AWE [1989]

Atomic Psalm

Last night the stars seemed not themselves,
for they sang such a lonely song
I heard all creation weep along.
And the moon seemed too molten hot –
it burned a hole right through the roof,
right through the sky, it burned
an empty place into the night.

And oh how the world rocked
like a cradle in the ether of the dark.
And how the children, lost in dreams,
awoke with a start, not out of fear
but from surprise. They blinked their eyes
in that starless night, that moonless night,
and cried, though no one heard.

God-Who-Is-Not, give us a lock
of your immortal hair, or give us stars
that we can reach and hang upon the bars
of our despair; give us back the rock
called moon, that still, white face
we write our lives upon. Give us back
our dark hope in its golden case.

Gary Snyder

⌒ SONGS FOR GAIA [1979]

Gaia

*(Frobenius: The Mother Goddess is the invisible
counter-player of Western Culture)*

Deep blue sea baby,
Deep blue sea.
    Ge, Gaia
Seed syllable, "ah!"

Whirl of the white clouds over blue-green
    bluegreen of *bios* bow – curve –
        cloud-gate, yün-mên

Chuang-tzu says the Great Bird looking down,
    all he sees is
        blue.

Sand hills. blue of the land, green of the sky.
    looking outward
    half-moon in cloud;

Red soil – blue sky – white cloud – grainy granite,
    and

Twenty thousand square hill miles of manzanita.
    some beautiful tiny manzanita.
    I saw a single, perfect, lovely,
        little manzanita.

        ah.

Primus St. John

Biological Light

We live here to eat;
Things stare at us.
Those things eat.
We call all of this hunger
The world.
Why?
Because we live here . . .

All over the world
Morning light is still happening
Like God.
It is so hard to tell
Who eats the plants first –
        Insect or crepuscular.

The wind feels the smallest birds
It's got.
If that is what we are,
It's not a lot –
Here comes the fox.

Noon: circles logically like the hawk.
God moves the rim around
Until the fox is in.
Now the fox is the hawk
And all the small things he ate
Believe him . . .

I have come here late;
The deer look like they have gone,
But thorns remind me
More is going on.

Gradually, memory sets the table back,
I have come from,
Across the water, as far back,
As I can know.
Friends there have eaten me;
Now I stand here, that torn by hate
As I myself have eaten them.

Late; the owls say *whooo*
For what more will surely come.
Finally, I am older –
But not enough –
Surrounded by what I know
Is falling back toward the grass
More like luck than hope . . .

I am just lying here
Thinking this is my sleep –
How cold it is outside.
If we were fish where it is very dark
It would all be so easy
Light would come from the dead things that we eat.

Kim Robert Stafford

⌒ A GYPSY'S HISTORY OF THE WORLD [1976]

Inside the Fence: Tule Lake Internment Camp

The violinist tamed the birds,
fastened branches on the wall,
offered crumbs between his whistling lips.
The children, when it didn't rain,
had to fill a hole with water
so they could see the sky ringed
by earth, their faces wind wrinkled.

Walking was the favorite sport,
finding things, bringing them back
to talk about over tea.
                              We live
this way still, though they say
the war is ended, we can go away.
They took the fences down.
                              Walking
is still the favorite sport, offering
a shoulder to any bird, watching the sky
in a puddle. Our faces wrinkle
for the old days, when we were confined.

William Stafford

British Columbia

After the border, it was trees all the way to
the end. When we talked to a native and
looked at his expression turned away, it was
trees. It was trees when anyone asked us
where we had been: land and land and land,
mountain by mountain, and everywhere.

We came to a lake so sudden that it
held a sharp outline in it, upside down:
the opposite shore offered us in the water.
And we waded in trees, drowned in them, held
there in the sky. I will never find enough
of the open again. I walk with my
family, carefully anonymous, hidden in trees.

Nancy Steele

⁓ TRACKING [1977]

Diminutive

1.

She extends the empty cup of her body.
He offers his ragged memory
the file of hungers
strung behind him like a breadline.

Years on that dole
what can ever be soothed?
Always the night
stretched so lean she sees through it.

2.

As if a woman should wear her sex
like a pocket with holes
spilling small change
or hang herself out for love like suet –

Whenever the stars
open their beaks,
her heart, without asking,
goes out to feed them.

Su Tung-p'o

⌒ SELECTED POEMS [1994]

Mid-Autumn Moon (1078)

Six years the moon shone at mid-autumn;
five years it saw us parted.
I sing your farewell song;
sobs from those who sit with me.
The southern capital must be busy,
but you won't let the occasion pass:
Hundred-league lake of melted silver,
thousand-foot towers in the pendant mirror –
at third watch, when songs and flutes are stilled
and figures blur in the clear shade of trees,
you return to your north hall rooms,
cold light glinting on the dew of leaves;
calling for wine, you drink with your wife
and tell the children stories, thinking of me.
You have no way of knowing I've been sick,
that I face the pears and chestnuts, cup empty,
and stare east of the old riverbed
where buckwheat blossoms spread their snow.
I wanted to write a verse to your last year's song
but I was afraid my heart would break.

Translated from the Chinese by Burton Watson

NOTE: In line 8, "pendant mirror" is a poetic term for the moon. The poem is addressed
to Su's brother, Tzu-yu.

White Crane Hill

AT MY NEW PLACE at White Crane Hill we dug a well forty feet deep. We struck a layer of rock partway down, but finally broke through and got to water.

Seacoast wears you out with damp and heat;
my new place is better – high and cool.
In return for the sweat of hiking up and down
I've a dry spot to sleep and sit.
But paths to the river are a rocky hell;
I wince at the water bearer's aching back.
I hired four men, put them to work
hacking through layers of obdurate rock.
Ten days and they'd gone only eight or ten feet;
below was a stratum of solid blue stone.
Drills all day struck futile sparks –
when would we ever see springs bubble up?
I'll keep you filled with rice and wine,
you keep your drills and hammers flying!
Mountain rock must end some time –
stubborn as I am, I won't give up.
This morning the houseboy told me with joy
they're into dirt soft enough to knead!
At dawn the pitcher brought up milky water;
by evening, it was clearer than an icy stream.
All my life has been like this –
what way to turn and not run into blocks?
But Heaven has sent me a dipper of water;
arm for a pillow, my happiness overflows.

Translated from the Chinese by Burton Watson

IN THE PREVIOUS YEAR the poet had bought some unused land at a place called White Crane Hill overlooking the Tung River in Hui-chou, and had built a house, which he completed in the second month of this year.

Line 24. "Arm for a pillow." An allusion to *Analects* VII 15: "The Master said, 'With coarse grain to eat, water to drink, and my bended arm for a pillow – I still have joy in the midst of these things. Riches and honor unrighteously acquired are to me as a floating cloud.'"

On First Arriving at Huang-chou

Funny – I never could keep my mouth shut;
it gets worse the older I grow.
The long river loops the town – fish must be tasty;
good bamboo lines the hills – smell the fragrant shoots!
An exile, why mind being a supernumerary?
Other poets have worked for the Water Bureau.
Too bad I was no help to the government
but still they pay me in old wine sacks.

Translated from the Chinese by Burton Watson

Line 8. "Wine sacks." Wine was a government monoply under the Sung, and lesser officials were
sometimes paid off in old sacks that had been used for squeezing wine, which could be sold or bar-
tered.

Robert Sund

Considering Poverty and Homelessness

(HOMAGE TO BASHŌ)

I cannot go back now,
   for what I have not done.
Of what is done,
take – and be kind.
   I am building a voice for my grief.
Alone, on foot,
if years from now I have learned anything,
   I will wander back.
Dust will rise up
on a dry winter road
where no one has walked before.

Karen Swenson

The Landlady in Bangkok

Because, separated from us by a language,
we find her a character without a plot,
a cotyledon without an ecosystem,
we invent her a husband, in the alley court,
a barren womb in this quiet cell of Bangkok's hive
under trellised vines in tin cans.

We graft invention on observation,
imagine her dispossessed
by a second wife's fecundity,
while she keeps her clothes in plastic bags
and sleeps upstairs on the corridor floor
before doors of the Spartan rooms she rents us.
We pass on hypotheses with other travelers' news –
names of hotels in Burma,
prices of guides in Borneo.

We know she counts herself to sleep with our money,
yet hoards notebooks grinning
with our faces which she forgets
with our comments she can't read.
But her records like our fabrications
are errant gestures around a kind of love.

She has no picture for our words for home
as we've no history for the wheal
of scar raised on her shoulder
as at the temple stairs she
buys piping sparrows in wooden cages
and frees them to gain merit –
each traveler fluttering
from Samsara to Nirvana.

Anna Swir

~ TALKING TO MY BODY [1996]

My Father's Workshop

I owe my second birth
to my father's workshop.
Father painted its walls
black, it was sublime
like a coffin, on the black walls
tall stained-glass panels
grew in corners, that was
power, they thronged,
every day taller, beating their wings
against the high ceiling, father
was painting in an overcoat, I was cold
and hungry, I used to sit
cross-legged on the floor,
we had no table, and I wrote
Latin verbs, in the alcove
the soup was boiling, mother,
sick, was lying there, I was
afraid she would die,
I would wake up at night
afraid they both would die,
I listened to their breathing, the window in the roof
was white with frost, the coal
used up, I thought
under my blanket that I
would be the Spirit-King, in the ceiling
there was a hook
from which a starving painter
who lived here
hanged himself.

*Translated from the Polish by Czeslaw Milosz and
Leonard Nathan*

A Bitch

You come to me at night,
you are an animal.
A woman and an animal can be joined
by the night only.
Maybe you are a wild he-goat,
or perhaps a rabid dog.
Hard to tell in the dark.

I say tender words to you,
you don't understand, you are an animal.
You are not surprised
that sometimes I cry.

But your animal body
understands more than you do.
It, too, is sad.
And when you fall asleep
it warms me up with its hairy warmth.
We sleep hugging each other
like two puppies who lost their bitch.

*Translated from the Polish by Czeslaw Milosz and
Leonard Nathan*

Arthur Sze

⌣ ARCHIPELAGO [1995]

In Your Honor

In your honor, a man presents a sea bass
tied to a black-lacquered dish by green-spun seaweed.

"Ah" is heard throughout the room:
you are unsure what is about to happen.

You might look through a telescope at the full
bright moon against deep black space,

see from the Bay of Dew to the Sea of Nectar,
but, no, this beauty of naming is a subterfuge.

What are the thoughts of hunters driving
home on a Sunday afternoon empty-handed?

Their conception of honor may coincide
with your conception of cruelty? The slant

of light as sun declines is a knife
separating will and act into infinitely thin

and lucid slices. You look at the sea bass's eye,
clear and luminous. The gills appear to move

ever so slightly. The sea bass smells
of dream, but this is no dream. "Ah,

such delicacy" is heard throughout the room,
and the sea bass suddenly flaps. It

bleeds and flaps, bleeds and flaps as
the host slices slice after slice of glistening sashimi.

The Great White Shark

For days he has dumped a trail of tuna blood
into the ocean so that a great white shark

might be lured, so that we might touch its fin.
The power of the primitive is parallactic:

in a museum exhibit, a *chacmool* appears as elegant
and sophisticated sculpture, as art, but

witness the priest rip the still-beating hart
out of the blue victim's body and place it

pulsing on a *chacmool* and we are ready to vomit.
We think the use of a beryllium gyroscope

marks technological superiority, but the urge
of ideologies then and now makes revenge inexorable.

The urge to skydive, rappel, white-water kayak
is the urge to release, the urge to die.

Diamond and graphite may be allotropic forms
of carbon, but what are the allotropic forms

of ritual and desire? The moon shining on black water,
yellow forsythia blossoming in the April night,

red maple leaves dropping in silence in October:
the seasons are not yet human forms of desire.

June Ghazal

Is the sun a miner, a thief, a gambler,
an assassin? We think the world

is a gold leaf spinning down in silence
to clear water? The deer watch us in the blue leaves.

The sun shines in the June river. We flit
from joy to grief to joy as a passing

shadow passes? And we who think the sun a miner,
a thief, a gambler, an assassin,

find the world in a gold leaf spinning down
in silence to clear water.

Parallax

"Kwakwha."
"Askwali."
The shift in Hopi when a man or woman says "thank you"
becomes a form of parallax.
A man travels

from Mindanao to Kyushu and says his inner geography
is enlarged by each new place.
Is it?
Might he not grow more by staring for twenty-four hours
at a single pine needle?

I watch a woman tip an ashtray and empty
a few ashes into her mouth,
but ah, I want
other soliloquies.

I want equivalents to Chu-ko Liang sending his fire ships

downstream into Ts'ao Ts'ao's fleet.
It does not mean
a geneticist must quit
and devote his life to the preservation of rhinoceros,
but it might mean

watching a thousand snow geese drift on water
as the sky darkens minute by minute.
"*Kwakwha,*"
"*askwali,*"
whenever, wherever.

T'ao Ch'ien

∼ SELECTED POEMS [1993]

Thinking of Impoverished Ancients

1.

The thousand things, and yet nothing
without refuge but lone cloud. In dusk –

vanishing into empty skies, into dusk,
when will last light ever grace it again?

flushed dawn sky breaking through last
night's fog, birds take flight together:

they venture carefully from the woods,
and wing home again well before evening.

Hoarding strength and guarding life apart,
how could anyone avoid hunger and cold?

If there's no one left who understands,
then that's that: what would you mourn?

2.

Bitter cold. The year ending like this,
I sun on the front porch, my coat closed.

There's nothing left of our south garden,
and dead limbs fills orchards to the north.

I try the ricejar: not a grain. I peer
inside the stove: no sign even of smoke.

It's late afternoon, classics piled nearby,
but I can't read in peace. The idle life –

it's not like Confucius in Ch'en, people
half-starved, but they're angry here, too,

and say so. Is there any solace? All those
ancients living this same enlightened life?

Translated from the Chinese by David Hinton

Elaine Terranova

⌣ DAMAGES [1995]

Self-Examination

He might be tethered
like an animal, kept from where
he wants to be. A big man,
nearing sixty. He sits and sweats,
though the room is air-conditioned.
His mouth a little open, he is reading
the sign on the door marked Radiology.
He is half up to go after her,

thinking of this life
of hers. The lapses in love –
his love – which cushions it.
The mutilating surgery and drugs
that sting the organism so it
draws back into itself, counterforce
to the disease, Whatever she has suffered
away from him in other rooms.

I pass easily where he
is not allowed. Like her, I'm chilled
in my thin gown. There is
a fineness, a definiteness
to her face. This beauty
is her own decision. A TV screen
plays a loop of film, women circling
their breasts with their fingertips,
women staring into a mirror.

A foam-rubber breast is lying
on a table. Each of us takes it
in turn, like a lump of dough
we must knead smooth. Something solid

stops me. Unyielding, jewel-hard, a pebble
in this mud. Such seeds grow.
I touch the hollow between
my breasts, this emptiness
that is in me a sign of want.
I look at our still-dressed hands.
Watches, rings. What do they have
to do with us? – madly flashing in the light.

Cheryl Van Dyke

⌒ CHEAT GRASS [1975]

Birth, 1975

I remember the birth
of my daughter
and why each summer
my fingers swell
tight as new buds
kept from their blossom
our attempt to prevent
their leaves from falling

and I listen
to the soft cries
of my daughter
as she tumbles
in her sleep
fingers clutching
the night wind
of all her memories

which dreams
will she remember
when she has children
the counting of summers

and why the selection
although time is an answer
unobtainable
even at its passing

Xavier Villaurrutia

⌢ NOSTALGIA FOR DEATH [1993]

Nocturne: The Eternal

When men straighten their shoulders and go by
when they let their names drop away
till even the shadows show shock

when a dust finer than smoke
clings to the crystals of a voice
and the skin of faces and the skin of things

when eyes shut their windows
to the rays of the prodigal sun, preferring
blindness to forgiveness, silence to sobbing

when life or what we uselessly call life
when it arrives with its unnameable name
undresses to leap into bed
and drown in alcohol or burn in snow

when I when if when lie when life
wants to meekly surrender in the dark
without even naming the price of its name

when a few forgotten stars still shine
in the loneliness of the dead sky
and the silence of silence is so vast
we wish it could speak

or when a mouth that does not exist
screams an inaudible scream
that showers our faces with living light
then flickers out, leaving us deaf and blind

or when everything has died

so hard so slow we're terrified
to raise our voices and ask "who's left?"

and I doubt I should answer
that unspoken question with a scream
for fear of discovering I no longer exist

for perhaps my voice too is no longer alive
except as a memory in my throat
and it is not the night but loneliness
that fills our eyes with shadows

for perhaps the scream is the presence
of an ancient world
an opaque speechless word that suddenly screams

for life silence skin and mouth
solitude memory sky and smoke
are nothing but the shadows of words
to hold back, for us, the night

Translated from the Spanish by Eliot Weinberger

Emily Warn

〜 THE LEAF PATH [1982]

Dwelling

Outside a rain steady and hard as nails
knocks at the first plum blossoms
to brush February's dull grey.
All winter I have come to this empty house
in mid-afternoon, to this quiet,
begging to be silenced by you.
I cook dinner at three,
blinding the windows with steam,
or bury myself in books
fighting the impulse to curl into a seed
dormant until your return.
Occasionally, I rouse myself to walk in the rain
past the gully, the alder's red haze
decorated by ghost globes of nests
and last year's purple clematis flowers.
Each morning it is more difficult
to face the round of emptiness and desire.
One dawn they will find us,
our legs spiraled as morning glory,
our bellies warm,
and our eyelids fluttering,
a rippling sheen of birds.

After Reading the Book of Splendor

A cloud hides the sun. A photograph
of a weathered boathouse on an empty beach
illumines the room. It has become itself over time,
sitting slightly off-square, hunched
over its vacant slip. Patches of moss
slant like rain on the steep shake roof.
The boathouse casts a shadow on the white sand
that is a door, a place for the eye to rest
after staring at the brightness
of the blank sky. Its other door never shuts.
It waits before the sea for the old wooden lorries
to return. There are no boats on the waves. No kelp
or driftwood on the beach. Just the boathouse,
doors unlatched.

Kathleene West

~ LAND BOUND [1978]

To My Twin Sister Who Died at Birth

Never did I learn to share. Expanding
the womb with my fat kicks, anticipating the rush
to the picnic table for home-frozen ice cream,
sneaking the wishbone from the Thanksgiving platter,
the unsuccessful nights flailing out
my portion of a bed, I cramped you, small
and thin. Now, pausing before a mottled rock
to chisel my daughter, I imagine
a woman who lives.

When Aunt Bakie brought the silver dollars,
you smiled and bounced.
I cried under the coffee table.
The same temper, the passion for chocolate,
but long after you've flared
and forgiven, I pout
and plot disasters
for Dr. Dalton and the allergy shots.
Never soap under the fingernails to stop
your nibbling! Never pacing the rug
for lack of a smoke!

From Mazatlán and lover, you send pieces
of the novel in progress, self-portrait
of a woman who loves easily and for years.
Mornings, I shiver a glance to the mirror
and wonder how you look,
but you won't leave the sun and I'm held
by the iron rays of the rain. Next month
a birthday. Did you live
to hear the slap, my howl?
I share it with you now.

By Water Divined

A pebble ripples the lake,
disturbs its determined smoothness.
Long after the small stone sinks
into the anonymous mud,
the lake shudders, convulsing upon itself.
Which is more beautiful?
The placid surface or the water that wavers,
transforming the image of a woman who leans
over the edge to watch the water stretch
then settle her features.

Still as the air she holds.
If a breeze whispers its way across the water,
it busies itself away from her,
leaving the fall of hair,
the drape of her clothing
in one smooth meld.
She remembers yearning for wind,
wind to scrape dry her cheeks
when the man with the fine guitar
plucked at her heart.

But as her tears dried
so did her heart.
The wind eroded her
like a poorly-tilled field
and she learned to wish for rain
and speak of crops, their yield separating
the good years from the bad.
She fears for the winter wheat, tempted
by unseasonable sun to appear too soon.
No human act can save it.

Still, she allows herself this indulgence,
makes pilgrimage to the lake,

man-made, shallow,
but water enough to imagine
another geography, another kind of strife.
She splashes her face and waits
for wind and water to meet at her lips.
She has grafted herself to this land
where the cycle turns on the harvest,
not death.

A last look at the water lifts her spirit,
reassures her that she shares
the ache of return with earth and weather.
Her breath quickens
and she sings, her voice a counterpoint
to the regularity of rise and fall,
the lone melodic line of plainsong,
a chant to celebrate the continuous ritual
that enters her words
that survives without her
that she sings.

Michael White

Recurrence

Darkness, but
a mountain wind howled through the canyons,
through the dark-red willows bent wildly about
along the snowy banks – whining and drowning out
the sound of rapids hurtling, gnawing away at rock
and root, and the sounds the spruce made creaking: strokes
of cadmium blue on white. And somehow what
occurred to me, as it flew above
the phosphorus light-gray foothills at the ends
of streets, was a page of newsprint rising suspended
over the rooflines – flown on the gusts that dragged me from
a vivid sleep, absently stripping a frond
of the window fern in my hands. And the smoke-fog
was flushed from the back streets where it lurked
all winter, as a last haze of leaves flocked
suddenly up from the skeleton poplar,
and that hollow wailing honed against the edge
of things, against the parked cars
filmed with salt, and the darkened houses.

Already then, the white-gold skies of
January seemed an hallucination;
but spring was still holding off, and the air
was so thickly wound with dust that children might not
have known their own front lawns (such as lawns were)
if they hadn't left wagons or robots out
in random, upflung attitudes of exultation.

This scene coalesced in a minute or two,
as a window somewhere upstairs shook hard
in flurries, until I remembered your voice
on the phone: its emptiness, its limp indifference to

the crushing words you whispered.
                              (All night I dreamt
of a river swept with gestures of mist,
with shadowy overhanging branches mirrored in it, blurred
a little in the barest riffles swirled
downstream like a tremor across a face. Nothing was sure
in that slow body of sky-filled current,
not the sound of your voice in the silence, or
the watery shapes of trees on the opposite shore,
not even the opposite shore.)

And *that* was an ordinary day at last. The heavy light
in half-mile splashes let through gaps
in the Wasatch, fell through the ghost-gray aspen,
caught on the first of the gray-green roofs, as if
all that could happen here had happened.
And before I left, the sky made up its mind
abruptly, shearing open over the sandblown reaches
I would drive that day, where mesas and sandstone reefs
rose at me like a storm at sea that crests
beneath the weight of wind.

And suddenly, the steel-bright air
was locked in its late thaw, and everything thin –
lamp posts, flagpoles, spires of pine –
dissolved like salt in the chill March glare.
Waves of rust and amethyst throbbed up
the broken sky. How could I understand
that nothing can save you? Soon
the deep-bass Catholic bells downtown would blend
with the lisp of traffic, and crocuses would bloom,
next week, across the faded neighborhood
like a shot of clear snow water,
but I couldn't think, as panic loomed,
of that white hush, of what could hide
so long, love, in the blood.

Eleanor Wilner

Meditation on the Wen Fu

When the heavenly Arrow is at its fleetest and sharpest,
what confusion is there that cannot be brought to order?

Lu Chi speaks of the heavenly arrow
and the sky parts. Quietly: not
with the flourish of trumpets, nor
with the clang of bronze doors thrown back, nor
with the velvet pomp of the lifting curtain – but
with the almost invisible shift of a cloud
that had obscured the sun, or the way
the dusk melts slowly into dark
and the stars ignite. This is not
the firing of an arrow, but merely
the drawing of heaven's bow.

It is hard to draw, and harder yet to say.
For this the brush had to be
invented, to speak in a wet rush like the living
tongue, moving over everything as a stream licks over
stones, in love with the feel of what
is opposite, or meeting another stream
with the lush music of affinity, or
after a long coursing through the rock beneath
the earth, it cries up
into the light, as a fountain.
As to the flowing and the not-flowing,
no one can explain it: how the spring
that gentled the earth with moss
and drew from it the delicacy of ferns
suddenly dries up
as if the voice of a god were stilled.

And the dead ferns rest brittle underfoot,
the dry moss answers the hand with the scratch of briars,
making it a place now for the tourist,
for the disappointment of cameras. Though,
now and then, one comes who imagines
she hears in the sighing of wind in the dry weeds
some spirit released – a bird sprung from a trap.

While, in some unmarked spot, sacred
to no tribe – a trickle begins in the rocks, and,
in the slow way vision alters from below,
a pool takes shape like a quiet eye
to hold the heavens in its gaze, the sky
looking up through floating leaves,
having found its proper home.

And, as to the heavenly arrow
of which Lu Chi speaks – it must have struck
straight down, deep into stone, into the heart
of granite. Strange, then,
what wells up, what pours forth in a flood,
should be both clear and bright
as water, heavy and dark as blood;
that stone be wounded into speech
and that such wounds should heal us.

The Muse

There she was, for centuries, the big
broad with the luscious tits, the secret
smile, a toga of translucent silk, cool
hand on the shoulder of the suffering
poet – the tease who made him
squeeze those great words out. He
was the mirror *and* the lamp, she the torch
who burned with the blue butane of a pure
refusal, too good for mortal use; her breath
was cold as mountain streams, the chill
of the eternal – no hint of plaque

or any odor of decay. Ethereal as hell,
a spirit in chiffon, the mystery is
how she had got so rounded in the butt
and all her better parts as soft as butter,
why such a wraith should be so ample,
what her endowments had to do
with that for which she set example –
all this was surely Mystery, oh that elusive
object of desire, that "untouch'd bride
of quietness," that plump poetic dish
who lived on air but looked
as if she dined on pasta.

Basta!
A pox on the great Lacan,
who writes with his eraser, on all poetic
Graces, mute and pensive, concave exactly
where he is most extensive – oh look
what she has *not* that he has got,
a thing I'm too polite to mention
except to say it rhymes with Venus,
it was the Latin word for tail;
its root, therefore, is *not* the same as pen,
which comes from the word for feather.

But enough of these fine distinctions.
What a great tradition was born when
Alexander whipped his penknife out, cut
the knot she carefully had tied, leaped
on his mount, a perfect straddle
and let the crotch decide
who was the horse and who was the rider,
who was the muse and who
the writer.

Conversation with a Japanese Student

That lovely climbing vine, so fresh
at dawn, so shy at noon, whose blue
countenance we call Morning Glory, you
call it *asakao*, Morning Face.
"What is this glory?" you ask, child
of *akarui*, even the memory of war
effaced. "What is it all *for?*"

＊

Here is an artist working, his brush
is history's tongue, his canvas
allegorical and large, the landscape
must be ample for his theme –
the turn of epic tides, pulled
in the wake of a dream, Glory,
unlike her homely twin, Mortality,
casts no shadow, never rests
("A beautiful and charming Female
floating Westward through the air,
bearing on her forehead
the Star of Empire"). There,

notice that Glory is artfully draped
in a tunic of pale silk in the Classical style
her limbs as plump and supple
as oil paint and appetite
can make them, the lift of her head – proud,
a summons and a dare, one delicious arm
carries a bright banner streaming in the air
its design illegibly wrought
with large suggestions. But of Glory
you can be sure because
an army marches in her train
almost a shadow, darkening the land.
At times, a peasant woman
raising her gaunt baby in a trite appeal
may momentarily block the light, obscure

Glory, put a little in the shade
all that golden beauty
the toss of whose curls is worth
a thousand ships, a million
villages, the world

for even a glimpse, the faintest rustle
of the hem of Beatrice's skirt
as it disappears around the corner
of the gates of pearl to the eternal
harbor, the flutter of doves
in the white thighs of Helen, desire
in its perfected form. The mirror of art
becomes a burning glass in the light
of absolute desire, the brush a flame
about to be consumed, for he has reached
the limits, here, of art – as Michelangelo
one night when he was old, in his rage
at the stubborn stone's refusal
to yield to his conception, attacked
his last Pietá with his chisel
trying to tear the pattern from the matter,
Christ from the arms of his grieving
mother; his servant
was forced to subdue the master
in order to save the work.

This time, no servant to intervene
and fire at the core, the center
split – as if mankind, with its cold
forever mind, trapped in its furious, failing heart
had torn the Pietá apart from within – gone
the mother, a cloud of glowing dust,
gone the son, dissolved
in the monstrous cloud, heaven's fungus
growing on the axis of the world
casting its white shadow on the hills
pitiless as any parasite
whose life depends
on what it slowly kills.

No brush can paint a light so pure
  only the blind can see white hot
 it whites out everything but what is not
  the sun's high noon, but brighter . . .
"ex Occidente, lex; ex Oriente, lux"
 out of the West, law; out of the East, light.

   *

At Nagasaki in the Peace Park near
the epicenter of the blast
there is a glade
so dense with foliage, bushes, asakao
and pine, you'd almost miss the sign, hand-drawn,
the only one in English that I saw:

THEY SAID NOTHING WOULD GROW HERE FOR 75 YEARS

And though the language was my own
I found it difficult to read
through such a thick exquisite screen
of evergreen
and tears.

The Secret Garden

The way you see it first is through
the keyhole, that aperture with hips,
and one you have to crouch down low
in front of, and squint to get a look
inside. A green space glows, oh it is
pretty, as aqueous as an aquarium,
where slender shapes, finned and neon-
spotted, glide beside your eyes, and press
their tiny noses to your glasses. Lean
closer, the keyhole holds the Mystery, until
of course, a key's inserted and spoils
the view. Meanwhile, the green invites you:

rosehips, clinging vines, the shy nasturtium,
grapes by the pound, diminutive white lilies
of the valley, pussy willows; in the shade,
moss, moss on every stone, moss crawling
the walls, moss over roots, soft, smothering
moss – underneath it all: a million worms,
brown, segmented, one end like the other,
a poem that ends with its opening line.

When it rains in the secret garden,
the worms come out and sport; they push
their wet way through the parting
particles of soil, they slip through mulch
and lift their small snub noses, faces
empty of expression as a toe, and lo,
they dance among the fallen petals, cavort
in the brackish puddles, splash and writhe
until the garden is alive with coils
and coils of shining brown (a python
if you think of them together) – until
the earth itself is pure Medusa, lost
head of blue spinning through the vacant
cosmos, its crust a fume of writing
serpents . . . and that, dear Jack,
is what is in the secret garden:
you are invited to come in for tea. But
bring your own cup and a folding chair,
and do wear rubbers, as there is danger
of infection, and we should hate
to think the worms could get you
before we're through with tea.

Marianne Wolfe

~ THE BERRYPICKER [1973]

The Thaw

Late in November
The morning sun shows the trees
In white against white.
There is a certainty that
Tomorrow will be the same.

For months thereafter
The days hang onto each other
Like timid sisters.
Nothing is changed but bed sheets
Where I lie white against white.

I move out of the solitude,
Attaching myself
To some sight or sound,
Wrapping myself in it
Like a cocoon inside a leaf.

Then one day in April
The branches of trees claw
At the passing clouds,
And the spaces between
Are filled like lungs in the thaw.

The days move quickly,
Bicycles coasting downhill,
And I wonder if
I am standing still
And the landscape is moving forward.

In the transition I emerge
As if from a cocoon, renewed;

Perhaps nude, I continue
Though no more beautiful
And knowing no more than before.

Robert Wrigley

The Sinking of Clay City

When the last mine closed
and its timbers turned pliable as treesap,
the town began to tilt, to slide
back into its past like a wave.

Old men, caught by the musk
of seeping gas, arrived at the mainshafts
hours before dawn. Their soft hands
turned the air like handles on new picks.

Here and there a house split,
a cracked wishbone,
and another disappeared like crawlspace
behind a landslide.

So the townspeople descended the sloping entrances,
found them filled with a green
noxious water. Each drank a little
and forgot about the sun.

Some dug at rusted beercans
or poked at a drowned rat, more patient
than dedicated archaeologists,
and waited for their other lives to join them.

Yoshihara Sachiko

Air Raid

When people were being killed
how could the sky have been so beautiful?

I had never seen such a gorgeous sunset.
Even the clouds were going up in flames.

When I crawled out of the shelter
a fragment of the night sky hissed obliquely by my ears.
Overwhelming light flared in eight glass windows,
one color fighting against another,
all reflected sumptuously as on a screen –

the red struggling to redeem
the blue of day from the black sky,
purple looming, green dashing, orange flowing,
colors of all kinds mixing, shrieking –

was it the southern part of the city
that was bathing in golden rain
falling brightly, god knows from where?
Was it an alien world enclosed within the glass?
Was it silent, dark, heated air
that whirled about, encircling
the dumbfounded little Nero?

How could a war have been
so beautiful?

Translated from the Japanese
by Naoshi Koriyama and Edward Lueders

Yuan Mei

∼ SELECTED POEMS [1997]

Writing What I've Seen

All things that live
must make a living.
There's nothing got
without some getting.

From fabled beast to feeble bug
each schemes to make its way.
The Buddha, or the Taoist sage?
Unending in his labor;

and morning's herald, the rooster, too
can he not cock-a-doodle-do?
I hunger, so I plot to eat;
I'm cold, and would be robed . . .

But great grand schemes will get you grief.
Take what you need, that's all.
A light craft takes the wind
and skims the water lightly.

Translated from the Chinese by J. P. Seaton

Old and Traveling

At my age to go ten thousand miles
I will admit, takes gall.
Singing toward a thousand peaks
I sometimes shy away.

But I would add that notable peaks

share this with noteworthy men:
only a fool, having met with one,
will not find it hard to part.

Translated from the Chinese by J. P. Seaton

On the Road to T'ien-t'ai

Wrapped, surrounded by ten thousand mountains.
Cut off, no place to go . . .
Until you're here, there's no way to get here.
Once you're here, there's no way to go.

Translated from the Chinese by J. P. Seaton

Last Poem: Goodbye to My Garden

Was I no more than some fairy being,
strange beast from the Sutra of Ceylon,
arisen and set free to play
in Hsiao-ts'ang's summit garden?

Did I not know that garden's guests
of poems and lutes, wine and songs
would also hear the gong of time,
the last dripped drop of the water clock?

My eye roams the towers and pavilions,
and I know these lines are my farewell.
This mountain full of birds will stay,
forever wound and bound in its flowers.

Long ago an Immortal chose to return
to his home in the form of a crane,

and was almost shot down by a lad with a sling.
If I ever come back to this Paradise,
I'll remember to be careful.

Translated from the Chinese by J. P. Seaton

∽ NOTES ON THE BOOKS

The following is a roughly chronological bibliography of the titles published by Copper Canyon Press, with comments by the editor.

1973

GERALD COSTANZO
Badlands
The first book from Copper Canyon Press was also the first by Costanzo, who has gone on to write several award-winning volumes of poetry, most recently *Nobody Lives on Arthur Godfrey Boulevard* (BOA Editions), and to serve as Founding Editor of Carnegie-Mellon University Press. *Badlands* was printed with poems on recto only so there would be pages enough to bind with a spine; an edition of four hundred copies.

MARIANNE WOLFE
The Berrypicker
First poems by a twenty-one-year-old poet, illustrations by her sister, Tina Wolfe. Her sense of the line was derived from Levertov and the Black Mountain poets, but the transparency she achieved, her artlessness, is everywhere her own. A small paperback with a dust wrapper issued in an edition of five hundred copies. The Century Schoolbook type, in retrospect, was a very poor choice. Mea culpa.

SAM HAMILL
Heroes of the Teton Mythos
A draft of the first third of my long poem, *Triada*, this compact little book was set in Bruce Rogers's Centaur, a type I would come to love. Two hundred fifty paperbound copies.

W.M. RANSOM
Finding True North & Critter
The first book by a native Northwest writer probably better known now as a novelist, but he's still a fine poet. Ransom also began the Port Townsend Poetry Symposium and made it the best conference anywhere in the 1970s. The first edition was seven hundred fifty paperbound copies.

↜ 1974

JAMES MASAO MITSUI
Journal of the Sun
Another first book, this was also the first printed on the letterpress, from Tree Swenson's hand-set Baskerville type. Unfortunately a neglected poet, Mitsui is a high school English teacher whose second book was published by Graywolf Press. Issued in an edition of one thousand paperbound copies.

ROBERT HEDIN
Snow Country
The first of three books (one, *At the Home-Altar,* was a limited edition) by a poet then living in Alaska. One thousand copies paperbound; forty copies signed and hand-bound (over-bound in quarter leather) by Annie and John Hansen. Several other titles were similarly bound in tiny editions, many of which I no longer have, so must leave unrecorded.

JAMES BERTOLINO
Making Space for Our Living
The first of several books by Bertolino was issued in an edition of one thousand paperbound. He now lives in the Pacific Northwest and continues to publish widely.

HOWARD McCORD
The Old Beast
This suite of poems in a crusty persona was issued in an edition of one thousand paperbound copies. McCord has published dozens of books.

Copperhead One
This boxed set of fifteen broadsides was issued in December, on Kenneth Rexroth's birthday, and dedicated to my old friend. It includes Denise Levertov's poem "Voyage," which was the first Copper Canyon Press broadside, and her dedicatory note, along with contributions by Gary Snyder ("One should not talk to a Skilled Hunter about what is forbidden by the Buddha"), Robert Hedin, Van Dyke, Mitsui, and others. One hundred fifty copies. They represent our apprentice work on the platen press.

↢ 1975

CHERYL VAN DYKE
Cheat Grass
Once a promising young Northwest poet, Van Dyke is no longer "younger" and no longer publishes. This suite of poems was our first hand-sewn chapbook. Issued in an edition of five hundred copies.

W. M. RANSOM
Waving Arms at the Blind
The poet's second collection, a chapbook with his daughter's handprint used in the cover design. Five hundred hand-sewn copies.

SAM HAMILL
Uintah Blue
A small collection of shorter poems, a hand-sewn chapbook in an edition of two hundred fifty copies, most of which were given away.

Copperhead Two
This second boxed set of broadsides includes poems by Johannes Bobrowski, Alphonso Reyes, James Welch, Thomas McGrath, and William Carlos Williams's "Coda" from "Rogation Sunday," as well as Ezra Pound's translation of the *Ta Hsueh* or "Great Learning" of Confucius.

↢ 1976

T. E. JAY
River Dogs
The only published collection of poetry by this prominent Northwest writer, sculptor and foundryman, these terse imagistic poems were issued in an edition of one thousand paperbound copies.

GLADYS CARDIFF
To Frighten a Storm
The first book by a Native American poet from Browning, Montana, *Storm* was handset in Centaur type, but we had yet to learn to letter-space the capitalized titles. One thousand paperbound copies.

FRANK R. MALONEY
How to Eat a Slug
Another first book by a Northwest poet. Fifteen hundred paperbound copies.

PRIMUS ST. JOHN
Skins on the Earth
The first book by a remarkable Northwest poet whose recent books have been published by Carnegie-Mellon University Press, *Skins* was printed letterpress in an edition of one thousand paperbound and forty casebound, signed, and slip-cased copies. St. John would later serve on the Board of Directors of Copper Canyon Press.

RICHARD HUGO
Duwamish Head
Poems selected from the poet's out-of-print books, this chapbook was printed in an edition of one thousand copies from hand-set Centaur type on Curtis paper and handsewn in wrappers. I still think his early work is his best, and his clunking roughshod pentameter and deadpan delivery are, well, *funny.*

SAM HAMILL
The Calling Across Forever
The editor's second book-length collection of shorter poems (the first was *Petroglyphs,* Three Rivers Press, 1974). Paperbound edition of fifteen hundred copies; fifty signed copies casebound in cloth over boards with dust wrappers.

KIM ROBERT STAFFORD
A Gypsy's History of the World
Printed by the poet and Tree Swenson in an edition of one hundred signed, clothbound copies, from which fifteen hundred paperbound copies were printed photo-offset; the poet's first book.

KENNETH REXROTH
The Silver Swan
Poems from Rexroth's stay in Kyoto in 1974, I printed one hundred copies of this book in 18 pt. Centaur type on Rives paper. Two thousand copies were printed off-set and paperbound. This book contains Rexroth's epitaph: "The swan sings / In sleep / On the lake of the mind."

Copperhead Three
The third and final boxed set of broadsides includes Philip Levine's "And the

Trains Go On," and poems by Richard Hugo, William Stafford, Barbara Szerlip, Michael S. Harper, Gladys Cardiff, Robin Skelton, Madeline DeFrees, and others. One hundred fifty copies.

ᗭ 1977

NANCY STEELE
Tracking
The first (and only?) book by a fine young writer whom I met through the Artists-in-Education Program. The book was printed by Tree Swenson and an apprentice, Jo Cochran, from hand-set Centaur type on Curtis Rag paper and casebound in an edition of sixty signed copies, and in an offset trade paperbound edition of one thousand copies.

MARK PAWLAK
The Buffalo Sequence
Pawlak came to us at the recommendation of Denise Levertov, who wrote the Introduction. He has published several subsequent books. This one was issued in an edition of one thousand copies.

SAM HAMILL, EDITOR
Mid-winter Break-up: Poems from the Anchorage Poets in the Schools Program
This little anthology was produced for the program during the early part of my thirteen-year engagement with Alaskan education, teaching in cities and in remote villages and for ten years in the Alaskan prison system. Five hundred copies printed for Alaskan schoolroom distribution.

TOM REA
Man in a Rowboat
Rea's first book, a chapbook, was printed by the poet and Tree Swenson in an edition of five hundred eight copies. Following his apprenticeship here, Rea and his wife would found Dooryard Press in Wyoming.

THOMAS JOHNSON
The Ice Futures
Sixty copies were printed by Tree Swenson and Jo Cochran on Rives paper, signed and casebound; one thousand were printed offset and paperbound. I had virtually no contact with this poet. Widely published in the seventies, he remains a mystery to me.

MICHAEL CORR
To Leave the Standing Grain
Corr is a serious student of Zen, a remarkable woodblock carver whose work graces, among others, the cover of Gary Snyder's Pulitzer Prize winning *Turtle Island*. This collection of Zen-inspired poems and woodcut prints was designed and printed by Tree Swenson in an edition of one hundred signed clothbound copies, with a trade edition of one thousand printed photo-offset and paperbound.

⮌ 1978

DAVID LEE
The Porcine Legacy
Lee's first poems had come to me while we were still in Denver. By the time *Porcine Legacy* was ready for publication five years later, Lee had all but stopped writing his more conventional poems, finding his truest voice in these episodic poems filled with great good humor and shit-house philosophy. His first book, with illustrations by Dana Wylder, was issued in an edition of one thousand paperbound and fifty cloth copies.

ROBERT HEDIN
At the Home-Altar
The poet's second book was issued in an edition of one hundred signed, clothbound copies printed on Rives paper from hand-set Spectrum and Palatino Italic types with three drawings by Barbara Arnold. No trade edition was printed, as these poems would be gathered with others in *County O* (Copper Canyon Press, 1984).

GARY HOLTHAUS
Unexpected Manna
I had met the poet and historian during my travels in Alaska. This, his first book, contains an introduction by Gary Snyder, and was issued in an edition of fifty clothbound and one thousand paperbound copies. Holthaus has since published a second book (with Gibbs Smith).

KEN GERNER
The Red Dreams
One hundred copies of his first book were printed by the poet during an apprenticeship at the Press. The type is Kennerly, the paper Curtis Rag. One thousand copies were photo-offset from letterpress proofs and bound in paper. When last heard from, Gerner was a bookseller in Portland, Oregon.

TIM McNULTY
Pawtracks
Like Gerner before him, McNulty set his own type, also Kennerly, and printed seventy-five copies of his first book during an apprenticeship. One thousand copies were printed photo offset and paperbound. McNulty has since written several notable books on Northwest wilderness areas and continues to publish remarkable poetry. He still lives on the Olympic Peninsula.

KENNETH O. HANSON
Han Yü: Growing Old Alive
Kenneth O. Hanson is one of this nation's neglected treasures. A classmate of Carolyn Kizer's at the University of Washington, he is one of the most original of the old "Northwest poets" now in their sixties and seventies who studied with Theodore Roethke. Han Yü (768–824 CE)was the first of our many books bringing Asian poetry into American English. One of the great Ezra Pound scholars, Hanson retired from Reed College and presently lives in Greece. Alas, he no longer publishes. Issued in one thousand paperbound and fifty cloth copies.

NELSON BENTLEY
The Iron Man of the Hoh
Bentley taught and nurtured hundreds of novice poets during his teaching career at the University of Washington and hosted hundreds, if not thousands, of classroom poetry readings and workshops. He published several books of poetry. *Iron Man of the Hoh* collects his often hilarious apocalyptic poems. Issued in an edition of one thousand paperbound copies.

SAM HAMILL
Triada
This single poem of three parts, made up of three parts each (107 pages), deals with personal mythology and the history of the American West. We printed one hundred fifty copies on Rives paper from monotype Italian Old Style type (Dantesque?). We figured the fifteen hundred paperbound copies would last my lifetime; all these years later, I still think they may.

KATHLEENE WEST
Land Bound
Another apprenticeship, another first book. West printed sixty copies on Nideggen paper from hand-set Spectrum and Palatino types; one thousand were printed offset and paperbound for the trade. West has since returned to her native Nebraska, where she teaches and continues to write poetry.

TIM MCNULTY
At the Foot of Denali
A single poem; two hundred copies printed on the letterpress, sewn as a tiny pamphlet and given away. McKinley never saw Denali.

GEORGE HITCHCOCK
The Piano Beneath the Skin
Poems by the esteemed editor of *Kayak*. I don't know whether anyone has ever given ten seconds of thought to what George Hitchcock did for American poetry during the long run of *Kayak,* but I was honored to publish one of his books, the first from Copper Canyon Press in which the size of the edition is not stated in the colophon – probably one thousand paperbound copies.

EZRA POUND
The Great Digest of Confucius
I printed this tiny chapbook excerpt from the *Ta Hsueh* or *Great Learning* thanks to the kind permission of James Laughlin at New Directions. I wrote a brief preface printed on the endsheet before the title page and used Michael Corr woodblocks with the prose text. Type was Italian Old Style set by an apprentice, John Lane. One hundred fifty copies were printed on Rives heavyweight and sewn in wrappers and given away. I did this one just for the pure love of the text – the great teaching.

JOHN LANE
Thin Creek
A single poem by our former apprentice. Lane has since returned to his native Carolinas where he continues to write and publish poetry. He once sent me a small box of fossilized alligator turds, one of which we planned to mail to the annual winner of the Fossilized Alligator Turd Award for Poetic Mediocrity. The first turd went to Robert Bly as a Lifetime Achievement Award – sent with laughter and a bow. The rest were stolen by friends. Lane's first chapbook was issued in an edition of two hundred fifty copies from hand-set Palatino type, handsewn in wrappers.

ᕲ 1979

KATHLEEN ESTES
Omphalos
The first and only chapbook by this author, who apprenticed with the Press. An elegant little chapbook with a dust jacket; issued in three hundred fifty paperbound copies, many of which were never actually sewn or sold. Someone told me that she gave up poetry when she found God. God as Anti-Muse?

GERALD HAUSMAN
Night Herding Song
Poems by the author of *Circle Meadow* and other books. These clear simple poems reflect his life near Tusuque, New Mexico, where he built an adobe house. One thousand paperbound and fifty cloth copies were issued.

ROBERT WRIGLEY
The Sinking of Clay City
The first book by one of the Northwest's best younger poets, no longer young and now published in the Penguin Poets series, was designed by Tree Swenson and Kathleene West, and issued in editions of fifty cloth and one thousand paperbound copies. This book contains some of the best poems about mining and the miner's life to be found in our language.

BILL O'DALY
The Whale in the Web
Three poems by a co-founder of the press and revered translator of six volumes of late Neruda, handsewn in wrappers in an edition of two hundred fifty copies. O'Daly gave many years to editing *Willow Springs* at Eastern Washington University, and spent years at Miscrosoft; we're still waiting for his first book-length collection of poems.

GARY SNYDER
Songs for Gaia
We designed and printed a signed edition of this chapbook under the imprint of Kah Tai Alliance, and Sam Green (of Brooding Heron Press) bound about two hundred copies in cloth over boards, proceeds from sales going to a local battle to keep Safeway from building a "superstore" in our lovely little Kah Tai Lagoon in Port Townsend. We lost. Of course. Two thousand copies were printed and bound in wrappers for the press.

OLGA BROUMAS
Soie Sauvage
The second book by a poet whose first was winner of the Yale Younger Poets
Award. This one was described in jacket copy as "twenty short meditations on the
politics of love, on landscapes interior and exterior" and a long concluding mono-
logue. Born in Syros, Greece, Broumas is a Sapphic poet in ways to which others
may only pretend– intensely musical, politically fearless, she approaches the ec-
static. Tree Swenson and I designed and printed one hundred fifty clothbound
copies printed from hand-set Deepdene type on Rives paper. The first paper-
bound edition was two thousand.

DAVID LEE
Driving and Drinking
This book-length poem with the politically incorrect title should have earned
David Lee a truckload of praise and a pigpen full of awards. It tells the Odyssean
journey of one John Sims, gentle-hearted redneck roustabout and pig farmer in-
troduced in Lee's *Porcine Legacy.* From the building of the outhouse "whupper" to
the blood-chilling oil derrick fire that killed his friends and turned him to pig
farming, John is one of the greatest homespun American literary personalities
since Huck Finn. It is fierce, funny, serious, heartrending. A major opus. One hun-
dred copies were printed by the poet under Tree Swenson's tutelage, using Italian
Old Style type on Nideggen paper, signed and bound in cloth. A workday spent
making beer stains on the title and colophon pages: "Shall we give this one three
rings or four?" Two thousand copies were printed and bound in paper for the
trade in 1982.

SAM HAMILL, EDITOR
Yesterday's Faces: Washington State Poetry-in-the-Schools
Another anthology, hors de commerce, of poems by students for arts in educa-
tion. Kathleene West and I wrote a brief foreword and designed this little book.
Five hundred copies were distributed within the state school system.

SAM HAMILL
Reading Seferis
A single poem, designed and printed by Tree Swenson, sewn into wrappers made
from the trim from the cover paper for Olga Broumas's *Soie Sauvage.* My poem
commemorates an evening Broumas and I spent together reading the poetry of
the great Greek poet. Two hundred copies were (mostly) given away. I sent a copy
to Seferis's translator, Edmund Keeley, with a timid note apologizing for stealing
his (or Seferis's) poem; he wrote back that such a theft is the highest compliment,

so I went on stealing from him for the next ten years. Nine bows. I don't read modern Greek, but I can't imagine my life without Seferis. Or Broumas. Or Keeley. Such "thefts" of model and/or inspiration are every poet's real work – it is the real work of poetry to exist under conditions of personal appropriation.

THOMAS MCGRATH
Trinc
Tree Swenson and I designed and printed three hundred copies of McGrath's great ode to beer, one of his most famous praise poems. About two dozen were hand-bound in cloth, the remainder sewn in wrappers. Alas, no beer stains this time, just praise as only McGrath could praise.

BILLY MACK GAMMILL
Prune
This sequential "prose poem" in persona was printed by Tree Swenson in a letterpressed, signed edition of 100 copies. The author issued a small pirated paperbound edition at a later date.

↶ 1980

PAUL HANSEN
Before Ten Thousand Peaks
When I met the formidable scholar-translator-poet-painter, he was living in a float shack on the Skagit River, translating the poetry of ancient Chinese monks by kerosene light. He knows more about Chinese poetry than anyone I've ever met. He has published recent translations through Brooding Heron Press.

SAM HAMILL
animae
This was a very personal book for me, from Ed Cain's image of a fetus on the cover to the "family poems" inside. In a preface, I all but disavowed much of my earlier work in favor of a more universalist or feminist vision of my practice. It was also the last book of my own that I would publish in a commercial edition at Copper Canyon Press. It received a Pacific Northwest Booksellers Award.

WILLIAM KLOEFKORN
Not Such a Bad Place to Be
The former Nebraska State Champion hog-caller has spent a lifetime in Kansas

and Nebraska capturing the essence of small town life in the Midlands in this and several other award-winning volumes of poetry.

LEE BASSETT
Hatsutaiken
Hatsutaiken means "first physical experience," and Lee Bassett's prose-poems form a kind of tiny novel in chapbook format, each chapter or prose poem spoken through the persona of an adolescent. We issued this in a signed, hand-sewn edition of three hundred copies, Italian Old Style type on Rives paper.

SHEILA NICKERSON
Songs of the Pine-Wife
Sheila Nickerson, long-time resident of Juneau, Alaska, explores the sense of place – or what John Haines has called "the place of sense" – in forty-three interconnected lyrics. She has published several volumes of poetry and has been a constant contributor to the literary forum of the deep North.

MICHAEL CUDDHIHY
Celebrations
This large chapbook was designed and printed by Tree Swenson using Frederic Goudy's Italian Old Style type with Libra display type on Frankfurt Cream paper, handsewn into Fabriano wrappers in an edition of three hundred twenty-five. This was the first book for the esteemed editor of the influential *Ironwood*.

BELLE RANDALL
The Orpheus Sedan
This chapbook was issued in an edition of five hundred hand-sewn copies. Belle Randall had been a Stegner Fellow at Stanford University and had a previous book published by the University of Pittsburgh Press.

BARRY LOPEZ
Desert Reservation
A single three-page poem designed and printed by our apprentice, David Romtvedt, and Tree Swenson, three hundred copies were handsewn in wrappers. Whether this is the only published poem by the great naturalist, I cannot say, but it is certainly his first poetry pamphlet.

∽ 1981

JIM HEYNEN
A Suitable Church
Probably best known for his tales, *The Man Who Kept Cigars in His Cap* and *The Boys*, Jim Heynen has published several volumes of fine poetry. Presently teaching in Minnesota, he continues to publish poetry and prose. Issued in cloth and paperbound editions with illustrations by Barbara Arnold.

CAROLYN FORCHÉ
The Country Between Us
I designed and printed two hundred copies using hand-set Bembo type (some of it set by David Lee), designed by Aldus Manutius, on Rives paper, signed by the poet and handbound in five-piece cloth over boards by Marsha Hollingsworth. Such a fine and important book. But I still think the prose-poem about The Colonel should go.

ROBIN MORGAN
Death Benefits
We met at a conference for battered women where there were two hundred eighty women – and me. She has proven to be a major essayist and poet while maintaining (until recently) her editorial work at *Ms.* magazine. I designed and printed two hundred copies of this chapbook from Bill O'Daly's hand-set Deepdene type and sewed them into wrappers; forty signed copies were bound in cloth over boards by Marsha Hollingsworth, most of the proceeds from which went to the Jefferson County Domestic Violence Program.

WILLIAM STAFFORD
Sometimes Like a Legend
The poet and I selected from among a vast storehouse of poems connected in one way or another to the Northwest, and I designed and printed two hundred copies from Italian Old Style type on Nideggen paper, signed by the poet and bound in Canson paper and cloth over boards by Marsha Hollingsworth. Twenty-six copies, bound with Canson endsheets and lettered A–Z, contain a poem in holograph by the poet. The trees are Tree's.

DENISE LEVERTOV
Wanderer's Daysong
Two hundred forty copies of this slim book were designed and printed by Tree Swenson, using Bruce Rogers' Centaur type on Frankfurt paper. Ten copies were

printed on Hayle. All were signed by the poet and bound in cloth and paper over boards by Marsha Hollingsworth. Swenson had long wanted to print Levertov's poems. I, of course, did too. But I did not. Therefore, may I say once again, "This is a truly beautiful book in every way"?

EZRA POUND
From Syria
The worksheets, proofs, and text of a translation of the only extant poem by Peire Bremon Lo Tort, early Provençal poet. Robin Skelton provides a scholarly Introduction, placing the young Pound (in the year he graduated from the University of Pennsylvania, 1906) and his work in historical context. In *Spirit of Romance,* Pound ranks Peire Bremon the Twisted with Vantadour and Peire Vidal.

ROBERT SUND
The Hides of White Horses Shedding Rain
Three hundred copies of this chapbook were printed on Arches wove paper from hand set Bembo type, sewn into Rives wrappers, and signed by the poet. A selection of poems by the longtime Northwest poet and painter.

⤺ 1982

EMILY WARN
The Leaf Path
Selected by Susan Griffin as the winner of the King County Arts Commission (Washington) Publication Project, this is the poet's first book. She would spend fourteen years at work on her second (*The Novice Insomniac,* Copper Canyon Press, 1996), including a year as Stegner Writing Fellow at Stanford University.

MADELINE DEFREES
Magpie on the Gallows
DeFrees began publishing her poetry and prose while a Catholic nun, then left the order to teach, eventually directing the Creative Writing Program at the University of Massachusetts in Amherst. *Magpie on the Gallows,* her fourth volume of poetry, was issued in trade cloth and paperbound editions.

THOMAS MCGRATH
Passages Toward the Dark
This was the first of several major books by the late poet to be published by Copper Canyon Press. Robert Bly wrote of *Passages:* "This book contains some of the most marvelous poems ever written to children, the *Letters to Tomasito,* as well as continuations of *Letter to an Imaginary Friend,* by one of the great masters of the narrative in this century." McGrath was a World War II veteran, a Rhodes Scholar, a writer blacklisted during the McCarthy Era, and a lifelong revolutionary for whom poetry was both a source and a destination. Issued in an oversized paperback, it includes work reprinted from smaller books published by Holy Cow! Press and Uzzano Press. McGrath, in 1982, was almost completely unknown to younger generations of poets despite writing at the height of his powers and having already produced a substantial body of work. Issued paperbound.

DAVID LEE
Driving and Drinking
See entry under 1979. Photo-offset edition, sans original beer stains, of the letterpressed limited edition. A Dantean poem of our time. I hope I live long enough to see Dave Lee's poetry begin to get the attention it merits.

RICHARD SHELTON
A Kind of Glory
Tree Swenson designed and printed two hundred eighty copies from hand-set Centaur and Arrighi type on Ingres Antique paper, bound in handmade Diana cover paper by Marsha Hollingsworth, and signed by the poet. Shelton, who writes so passionately of the Sonoran desert, has published several award-winning books with the University of Pittsburgh Press.

MARK HALPERIN
A Place Made Fast
Of this second major collection of poems by Halperin, William Stafford noted that the poet "writes in the presence of earlier literature, and he contributes to that company by being himself worthy of it." Norman Dubie wrote, "Halperin's new poems are stopped elegies and life stories, little cataclysms of voice." Linda Pastan noted that the poems "are full of the narrative energy of people and places, real and dreamed, yet they never lose their lyric grace. This is an original and compelling book."

∽ 1983

OLGA BROUMAS
Pastoral Jazz
On the back cover, a photo of the author in sweatpants with saxophone. That about says it: sweet soul music. The jacket copy says she uses "healing and body-work skills to expand the capacity for ecstasy, memory, and expression." Formally educated in architecture and graphic arts, the architecture of her poetry resembles nothing so much as a great solo by John Coltrane or Ella Fitzgerald.

RED PINE
The Collected Songs of Cold Mountain
Red Pine (Bill Porter) was then living in Taiwan. Production of this book was nightmarish, frustrating for all concerned, and the book originally contained a small errata. But Porter's translation is splendid, and this bilingual cloth and pa-perbound edition has been a gratifying discovery for many who knew Han Shan (Cold Mountain) only through the two dozen translated poems by Gary Snyder, or the one hundred by Burton Watson. This one contains all 307 extant poems. See also Porter's translations of the *Tao Te Ching* and *The Zen Teaching of Bodhidarma* among many.

SAM HAMILL
Requiem
I set the Centaur type and printed two hundred fifty copies of this requiem *for* (but not about) my friend and teacher Kenneth Rexroth during the year following his death in June, 1982. I had begun the poem several years earlier, hoping to com-plete it before he died. The paper is Gutenberg Laid. The binding, cloth and paper over boards, is by Marsha Hollingsworth, and includes paper handmade by Sara Krohn from my old jeans. The tipped-in frontispiece is by Phyllis Hopeck and is printed on Kitakata paper. Probably my best work as printer-designer.

H.D.
Priest & A Dead Priestess Speaks
Two poems by the incomparable H.D. designed and printed in several colors from hand-set Bembo and Castellar types on Frankfurt paper by Tree Swenson; pro-duction includes illustrations adapted from Greek vase paintings – interior illus-trations by Swenson, the silkscreened cover image on Canson paper by Phyllis Hopeck from a screen by Drew Elicker. This is probably the most elegant book, in terms of production, that the press has produced.

KENNETH REXROTH
Fourteen Poems by O. V. de L. Milosz
"Oscar Venceslas de Lubicz-Milosz was born on the twenty-eighth of May, 1877, in Czereia, Lithuania... Much of his youth was spent in travel. When, in later poems and stories he speaks of the slums of London, the alleys of Hamburg, the ghetto of Warsaw, he speaks with accents of personal experience..." Rexroth writes in his Introduction to these poems translated from the original French. Czeslaw Milosz would say in his Nobel Lecture, "A new hierarchy of merits will emerge, and I am convinced that Simone Weil and Oscar Milosz, writers in whose school I obediently studied, will receive their due." I might say the same of Rexroth. Calligraphy by the incomparable Tim Girvin. Paperbound.

PABLO NERUDA
Still Another Day
This book was the first of six volumes of late Neruda poetry incomparably translated by William O'Daly. I set the Centaur type and printed two hundred fifty copies on Frankfurt Cream paper. The binding is cloth over boards by Marsha Hollingsworth, with Canson dust jacket. Jim Todd's wood engraved portrait of Neruda perfectly captures the elderly poet's melancholy tone: "I die with each wave each day. / I die with each day in each wave. / But the day does not die – ..." This is a poem of twenty-eight lyrics. A trade paperbound edition was issued the following year.

↩ 1984

ROBERT HEDIN & DAVID STARK, EDITORS
In the Dreamlight: Twenty-one Alaskan Writers
Publication made possible in part by a grant from the Alaska Humanities Forum and the National Endowment for the Humanities, this book was designed by Tree Swenson and issued in trade cloth and paperbound editions. "Place makes people; in the end it makes everything. Strong efforts may be made to deny the place, to silence the authentic, but the spirit of things will break through that silence... What we do and say here touches everywhere the common lot of people." – John Haines

PABLO NERUDA
Still Another Day
The trade paperbound edition of the 1983 title, this book was the first of many to

bear cover images by Galen Garwood, with whom I would collaborate on two books of interpenetrating poetry and visual art. Tree Swenson's design for this series was both beautiful and utilitarian.

CAROLYN KIZER
Mermaids in the Basement: Poems for Women
The subtitle is misleading. Every man should read "For Sappho/After Sappho" and "Pro Femina" and "Bitch" and all the other of these poems by the Pultizer Prize winner. The first of her books with Copper Canyon Press, the second being her "poems for men" (*The Nearness of You,* 1986), which carried no subtitle. John L'Heureux said it best: "The Greeks would have built her a temple." Issued in trade cloth and paperbound editions. The title is from Dickinson; the cover print by Jim Johnson; book design by Tree Swenson.

ROBERT HEDIN
County O
The poet's third book, excluding the *Dreamlight* anthology which he co-edited. He remains a very fine but neglected poet. I've always regretted that I couldn't have done more to bring his work the attention it richly deserves. Issued in paperbound only, with four monotypes by Galen Garwood.

DAVID LEE
The Porcine Canticles
More pigs, including those in the out-of-print *Legacy* together with new work. Tom McGrath told me, "Dave Lee's pig poems are the best thing to happen to animals in poetry since Kit Smart's cat." I always suspected a Ph.D. in Milton and training for the pulpit prepared Lee to meet his pigs nose-to-nose. They ain't metaphors! Issued paperbound only.

KATHLEENE WEST
Water Witching
The fourth book by the Nebraska poet includes the following perfect tiny "Poem for Lonely Grammarians: Copulative Verb Followed by Infinitive": "How clean it is / to be alone." Besides apprenticing at Copper Canyon Press, West worked at Abattoir Editions, and has been a Fulbright Fellow at the University of Iceland. Issued paperbound.

1985

Patricia Goedicke

The Wind of Our Going

A native New Englander who lived for fifteen years in Mexico, Goedicke presently teaches in the Creative Writing Program at the University of Montana, Missoula. This was her seventh book, and she has published several since. This one comes with high praise from Maxine Kumin and Hayden Carruth among others. Issued paperbound.

Ken Gerner

Throwing Shadows

The poet's second book features a thirteen-poem suite, "The Moon Year," a Pindaric dithyramb, and a deep sense of participation in the natural world. A fine book by a poet who has since published little. Issued paperbound.

Robert Bringhurst

The Beauty of the Weapons: Selected Poems 1972–1982

This is the first U.S. publication of a book first published by McClelland and Stewart in Canada. Bringhurst, who grew up in Montana, Wyoming, and Utah, has lived in the Middle East, Europe and Latin America, and for many years in British Columbia. The late great William Arrowsmith wrote of this book, "No doubt about it, Robert Bringhurst is the real right thing at last, a major talent." He is. He is also a major scholar of the history of typography and the printed book, and a scholar of several ancient and modern languages. That he remains virtually unknown in the country of his origin is shameful. Paperbound.

Pablo Neruda

The Separate Rose

These poems grew out of Neruda's visit to Easter Island in 1971. Alternating between the voice of "The Island" and the voice of "The Men," here Neruda attempts to recapture a prehistoric connection with nature. In O'Daly's luminous translation, one can hear the voice of the original. Paperbound.

Thomas McGrath

Letter to an Imaginary Friend, Parts Three & Four

The second and concluding volume of this major epic. The poet spent twenty-three years on Parts Three & Four, and the whole poem has been universally praised by poets as diverse as Diane Wakoski, Philip Levine, and Robert Bly. An oversized format was required to accommodate the poet's long (usually six-stress) lines and fit it as companion volume to Parts One & Two, published by Alan Swallow. *Letter to an Imaginary Friend* is one of the monumental achievements of our time.

VICENTE ALEIXANDRE
A Longing for the Light: Selected Poems
When he was awarded the Nobel Prize in Literature in 1977, Vicente Aleixandre was virtually unknown beyond the borders of his native Spain. His poems are in the Mediterranean tradition – full of light and darkness and a "song for the dawn of the world." This large bilingual selection of his poetry was edited by Lewis Hyde and originally published in cloth only by Harper and Row in 1979. Paperbound with a cover image from a monotype by Galen Garwood.

⟿ 1986

CAROLYN KIZER
The Nearness of You
The Pulitzer Prize winner's companion volume to *Mermaids in the Basement* (see under 1984) includes new work along with poems from out-of-print collections. Her "poems about men" bring Hayden Carruth, in his advance comment on the book, to quote Camus: "Classicism is nothing but romanticism without the excess." Another remarkable Jim Johnson print on the cover. Issued in cloth and paperbound editions designed by Tree Swenson.

RICHARD JONES
Country of Air
I had never heard of the poet and didn't connect him with his wonderful journal, *Poetry East,* when he read these poems at a gathering in North Carolina. Afterward, I asked whether he just might have a manuscript. David Ignatow wrote of this book, "To be able in simple narrative lines to convey the density and perplexity of living; to conceive a language capable of placing one in the presence of the thing itself; to realize that mastery over our lives we search for, if momentarily in the poem – this is art and there is nothing to compare with it or to surpass it. It is transcendence, and in *Country of Air,* Richard Jones has achieved it with saint-like dedication to his need." Paperbound.

MAURYA SIMON
The Enchanted Room
Of this, the poet's first book, Carol Muske wrote, "There are poems here that find the jewel in the lotus. They demonstrate most clearly a process that occurs throughout this book, a mysterious movement I much admire, by which the poet 'disappears' into the poem, leaving the reader with the pure moment, no shadow of a narrator...she is a prophet of the heart." Paperbound, the cover image is a detail from a collage by Baila Goldenthal, designed by Tree Swenson.

ODYSSEAS ELYTIS
What I Love: Selected Poems
Olga Broumas selected and translated these poems by the Greek Nobel Laureate. "If there is for each of us a different, a personal Paradise, mine should be inhabited by trees of words that the wind dresses in silver, like poplars, by men who see the rights of which they have been deprived returning to them, and by birds that even in the midst of the truth of death insist on singing in Greek and on saying, 'eros, eros, eros!'" The Sapphic Broumas reincarnates these surreal neoclassical poems perfectly. At the request of the translator, I provided an Afterword. Published in cloth and paperbound editions.

PABLO NERUDA
Winter Garden
This third volume of O'Daly's translations finds Neruda meditating on his own imminent death and the fall of his country's democratically elected socialist government, addressing both in poems that are among his best: "I owe to earth's pure death / the will to sprout." Published in cloth and paperbound editions.

SOPHOKLES
Philoktetes
The last play of the great Greek tragedian and author of the *Oresteia*, *Philoktetes* was written when Sophokles was eighty-seven, and is also the subject of Edmund Wilson's famous essay, "The Wound and the Bow." In the play, Philoktetes is bequeathed the magical bow of Herakles. In the company of Odysseus on the way to battle, he is bitten by a sacred serpent in a temple of Apollo, god of war. Odysseus, impatient with Philoktetes' cries, casts him ashore on the island of Lemnos, where the play unfolds. This translation, by Gregory McNamee, was the first in thirty years, and is easily the most cogent in our language. He captures the *poetry*. Paperbound.

ᔕ 1987

James Laughlin
The Owl of Minerva
J. Laughlin is a national treasure. The publisher of New Directions has perhaps allowed his personal modesty to overshadow his long distinguished life as the Catullus or Propertius of our time. From his famously eccentric lineation to his equally quirky wry observations, he is demonstrably a major talent. Issued in cloth and paperbound editions.

Pablo Neruda
Stones of the Sky
Published in Spanish in 1971, a year before his Nobel Prize and two years before his death, *Stones of the Sky* addresses the eternal metamorphosis of precious and semi-precious stone and crystal, common rock formation as they contain the secrets of mortality. Although not among the several books left on his desk at the time of his death and which O'Daly was translating, this late work seemed to fit into the late Neruda series because of theme and style, and James Nolan's translation captures the music and clarity of the original. Published in cloth and paperbound editions. Nolan's books of poetry, *Why I Live in the Forest* and *What Moves is not the Wind*, were published by Wesleyan University Press.

Jane Miller
American Odalisque
Her third major collection was her first with Copper Canyon Press. Jorie Graham wrote of this book, "She has managed a brilliant marriage between a poetry of process or open form and a poetry of finish, story and closure. I like to think of her work as that meeting ground where James Wright and Charles Olson find their common goals... She has developed a means by which to make chance contend with narrative; lyricism with cacophony and seriality." She teaches in the Writing Program at the University of Arizona, Tucson. Published paperbound, Swenson's cover incorporates Tom Wesselman's painting, "The Great American Nude #4," and it's unfortunate that we never sent a copy to Jesse Helms. Think of the free publicity a bald vulva on a book cover could generate from the Senate floor!

Robert Bringhurst
Pieces of Map, Pieces of Music
The second major collection by one of North America's most original and scholarly – in the best possible sense – lyric poets to be published by Copper Canyon

Press. Here, Bringhurst raises a Taoist mirror that reflects the living roots of poetry and thought even as it exposes our own age. Includes a "Cast of Buddhas, Ghosts & Other Creatures," and borrowings from and responses to some of the great minds of classical Asian wisdom-teaching. Paperbound.

JAAN KAPLINSKI
The Wandering Border
The major poet of Estonia, this is his second book in English, translated by the poet, Riina Tamm, and me (the first, *The Same Sea in Us All,* was published by Breitenbush Books in 1985). Kaplinski has translated from French, Spanish, English, Polish, and Chinese, and his poems reveal a kinship with Buddhist and Taoist poetry. His poetry has been highly praised by Denise Levertov and Gary Snyder, among others. Published in cloth and paperbound editions incorporating a sumi painting by George Tsutakawa.

SUSAN GRIFFIN
Unremembered Country
I had long admired Susan Griffin's poetry, which I had first read in fugitive publications by small presses, and especially admired her great poem-essay *Woman and Nature: The Roaring Inside Her* (Harper & Row, 1978) and her study, *Pornography and Silence* (1981). Tillie Olsen wrote, "In some of these poems, it is as if – through the thousand doors of death, of anguish – Susan Griffin entered, smelted in the crucible of our time – and somehow transmuted for us an integrative, a life-cherishing vision." Published in cloth and paperbound editions. Swenson's cover design incorporates Morris Graves's great painting "Machine Age Noise." Cloth and paperbound editions.

ᔕ 1988

JAMES GALVIN
Elements
This is the third book by the former National Poetry Series winner, the first with Copper Canyon Press. In my jacket copy, I noted that he is "equally at home with a fishing line or Euclid's geometry." Later, I would call him a Pre-Socratic. It's true. His poems are cut from hard ancient stone. Paperbound.

ODYSSEAS ELYTIS
The Little Mariner
This tour-de-force is the poet's first major work since winning the Nobel Prize in 1979. "Between the enigmatic 'entrance' to the book, and its closing gesture or 'exit,' the poet offers 'snapshots' from a life of 'chastely erotic travel' and a complex and profound field of experience comparable to his great *Axion Esti,* but far more accessible to the Western reader," the jacket says. Olga Broumas translated the book, and Carolyn Forché wrote the prefatory appreciation, noting, "This is a poetry of luminosity and resonance, clarity of soul, and deep transformative power. It cannot be imitated. Such work arises out of the language itself, and such a language out of the sea, the rocks, the history, and light of Greece, but arises only if such a poet as Elytis is present, and occurs in English only when a translator such as Broumas emerges to assimilate his labor." Paperbound.

THOMAS McGRATH
Selected Poems 1938–1988
Fifty years of the best of McGrath's remarkably various poems. Terence Des Pres compared him to Whitman. In my Introduction, I drew parallels with Tu Fu and Dante, to the poet's chagrin. "Throughout these poems, everywhere evident, is Thomas McGrath's great good humor, an astonished observer awed by beauty and sadness and *joie de vivre* – camaraderie found only in the hope for justice and in his fierce commitment to compassion and common good." A finalist for the National Book Critics Circle Award, *Selected Poems* won the Lenore Marshall Prize. Cloth and paperbound editions designed by Swenson, this cover is a personal favorite: her use of printing ornaments ("diapers") and type together with the poet's signature is very effective, the colors just right.

PABLO NERUDA
The Sea and the Bells
The sea is the "sound of stones being born," and the bells are those of passing ships, and in this book, one of eight manuscripts on the poet's desk at the time of his death in September, 1973, one finds Don Pablo's final poem, a love song for his wife, Matilde. *Bloomsbury Review* called it "A devastating sequence of poems written in Neruda's most biting, stark language and translated into a beautiful, hypnotic English." The fourth in the series of O'Daly translations continues the series with Galen Garwood's marvelous monotypes as cover images. Published in cloth and paperbound editions.

Carolyn Kizer

Carrying Over

Subtitled "Poems from the Chinese, Urdu, Macedonian, Yiddish, and French African," this volume is a selection of Kizer's work in translation – her thesis at Sarah Lawrence was on the influence of Chinese poetry in translation on the Imagists (and, by reference, herself). Some, like Bogomil Gjuzel, are unknown to North Americans; others, like Tu Fu, are much better known. Her "Pakistan Journal" in prose includes translations of poems by Faiz Ahmed Faiz, N.M. Rashid, and M. Safdar Mir. Her modern Mandarin is from the contemporary Chinese feminist Shu Ting. Published in cloth and paperbound editions with a remarkable wrap-around cover from the Korean painter Sin Yun-bok via Tree Swenson.

Jean Joubert

Black Iris

Denise Levertov's translations of poems from the poet's original French reveal a Rilkean spirituality in a world of sunlight and shadow, imaginary paintings, and supreme sensuality. His poems invoke and suggest and imply, searching for a human dimension beyond the physicality of the images themselves. Joubert, clearly a virtuoso, remains virtually unknown in North America. Published paperbound.

1989

James Laughlin

The Bird of Endless Time

Robert Creeley wrote of Laughlin's second book with Copper Canyon Press, "I think what most delights is the insistently human scale, the old-time Roman clarity of terms. But there is also that timeless intelligence of love's musing reflection, in whatever language impinges, or makes possible such ultimately human speech. In short, he's a gentleman and a scholar – and a poet of happily common places." Andrei Codrescu called him "the Catullus of *fin-de-siècle* America." Guy Davenport called his poems "victories of the heart," comparing Laughlin to Whitman and Dickinson. There's nobody at all like him. Published in cloth and paperbound editions.

Maurya Simon

Days of Awe

In the jacket copy I noted, "Her ear is alert to sophisticated cadences, sometimes metrically regular and at other times open, measuring idiom and phrase like a jazz musician exploring a chord progression. Vermeer's women, a rabbi's pants, nude mice – all sorts of things spark her poems, but it is her unique voice and vision which make them cohere." She continues to write and publish wonderful poems. Another beautiful cover image from Baila Goldenthal.

Stephen Berg
Crow with No Mouth: Ikkyu
Berg's "versions" of poems should not be confused with translation per se. They are poems based upon close readings by a deeply engaged poetic mind. They wrestle with the original philosophy that lies behind the writings of the incomparable fifteenth century Zen master-poet-calligrapher-musician and one-man cultural revolution. Issued paperbound with high praise from W.S. Merwin and Hayden Carruth. "This useless dying koan body singing its lust / weeds not yet cleared everywhere." I'd become a fan of Berg's "versions" with publication of *Nothing in the Word*, versions of Aztec poems (Mushinsha, 1972). Swenson's design of this little book is striking.

Olga Broumas
Perpetua
I wrote in the jacket copy, "A native of Syros, Greece, she speaks as poets must – as an exile, claiming the world as her intimate listener. Stubbornly refusing to surrender the dignity of erotic engagement, the dance of the intellect among the things of this world, the body's coming to awareness of spiritual depth, her poems extend a broad social empathy where joy and sadness, hope and despair, coexist in perfect harmony." Published paperbound.

Jerome Rothenberg & Harris Lenowitz, editors
Exiled in the Word:
"Poems & Other Visions of the Jews from Tribal Times to Present," explores, through a collage-style poetic, sources from ancient Hebrew to Edmund Jabes, from the *Talmud* to Paul Celan, from the *Zohar* to Zukofsky. This is a wealth of poetic treasure and lore with commentaries by Rothenberg, whose work in ethnopoetics has been as acclaimed as his own poetry. Published paperbound, the cover image is from a painting by one of our resident grammarians, Laura K. Popenoe. The artist added gold Hebrew letters to the image for use on the book.

Ou-Yang Hsiu
Love & Time
J.P. Seaton's sparkling translations of (mostly) love poems by the great self-edu-

cated Ou-Yang Hsiu (1007-1072), one of the preeminent literary figures of the Sung dynasty. His collected works fill one hundred fifty-three volumes. Alas, somewhere in production Swenson's design of this little book ended up with a washed-out look. Jacket copy is all but impossible to read. The poems, and the book's interior, shine. Published paperbound.

ᕔ 1990

DAVID LEE
Day's Work
More tales of John Sims and pigs and broken fences, including some marvelous longer poems. This book won the Publication Prize of the Utah Original Writing Competition. His fourth book with Copper Canyon Press, and he was finally getting recognition in his own back yard. The cover of this paperback has a wonderful wood engraving, by Michael McCurdy, of a farmer and farmhouse in low light. Morning or dusk?

THOMAS CENTOLELLA
Terra Firma
Selected for publication in the National Poetry Series by Denise Levertov, Centolella's first book reveals a poet with remarkable maturity and a range of skills, most notably for combining the lyrical with the narrative impulse. She wrote, "Rich in metamorphic illuminations of concrete detail, their diction colloquial but not constrictive, Thomas Centolella's poems are sensuous, humorous, passionate, and compassionate." Published paperbound.

HAYDEN CARRUTH
The Sleeping Beauty
In 125 verses, Carruth proves himself a virtuoso of improvisation within form. Carolyn Kizer wrote of this epic meditation, "The poem is unique in its understanding of the link between love of woman and love of nature. Those two great contemporary issues, recognition of women, and respect for our fragile world, are bound together in profound unity." This is a revised edition of a poem originally published in 1982. Carruth's first book with Copper Canyon Press was published paperbound.

MARVIN BELL
Iris of Creation
Bell's quirky, lively imagination and idiomatic language admit to a plethora of in-
fluences and experiences, articulating the need for perpetual transformation from
within. His poems spring from the meeting of the sacred and the profane, from
the mundane and the phenomenal, often lending definition to those qualities of
life which most defy definition. The prolific poet's first book with Copper Canyon
Press was published in cloth and paperbound editions.

PABLO NERUDA
The Yellow Heart
The fifth in William O'Daly's translations of late Neruda, *The Yellow Heart* was
written as the poet prepared for his own death by cancer while an imminent U.S.-
backed military coup was taking root in his native Chile. O'Daly writes in his In-
troduction, "He came to see poetry as a moral act, with personal and communal
responsibilities. A poet's investiture is to remember where we came from and to
ask who we are, to ask who we are as a community and where we are headed. . .
Neruda believed poetic form to be as dynamic as the process of transformation
and discovery." Poignant, self-effacing, humorous, and sacred, these last poems by
the Nobel poet reveal his eternally restless imagination, his passionate love of life,
and his courageous acceptance of death. Cloth and paperbound editions.

DAVID RAY
Not Far from the River: Poems from the Gāthā Saptaśati
Half of the seven hundred verses written two thousand years ago in Prakrit, a
peasant dialect of Sanskrit, translated by poet David Ray, these quatrains explore
the erotic life. Ray writes in his Introduction, "The passions of lovers and seekers
of wisdom a full twenty centuries ago were as immediate, as recognizable as our
travails and tortures, our joys and our self-deceptions. . . The scenes these verses
immortalize endure. A thousand years hence, they will still be reenacted." Pub-
lished paperbound.

↪ 1991

KAY BOYLE
Collected Poems
Although renowned for her two dozen volumes of fiction and several of nonfic-
tion, Kay Boyle's poetry was not at all well-known to younger generations of poets

and readers despite five previous volumes. Her poetry, like her prose, locates the political within the personal, the imaginative act within a historical context. A reviewer for *Choice* wrote, "She shows her extraordinary capacity for entering into the lives and tragedies of others. In writing about Attica, about the Colonels' takeover in Greece, about the abuse of American Indians, the courage of women, political murder in Iran... she succeeds in writing in language that is rich and varied, eloquent and elegiac." Published in cloth and paperbound editions.

THOMAS MCGRATH
Death Song
Facing – and ultimately embracing – his own imminent death with a song, Thomas McGrath celebrated life more nakedly, more enthusiastically, than any American poet since Whitman, reaffirming our interconnectedness with one another and with the natural world. McGrath left a request that I edit this posthumous book, selecting from a large manuscript which often had variant versions of a poem from which to choose. The Introduction is by Dale Jacobson. The poet had asked us to use the cover image, a striking little singing angel beside a tombstone; painted by Charles Thysell, it is entitled "Poesis."

RICHARD JONES
At Last We Enter Paradise
The poet's second volume of poetry is rooted in the redemptive powers of awareness and acceptance of loss as he transforms melancholy experience into consoling songs. With a strikingly delicate touch and understated elegance, Jones elevates mundane events into the realm of Paradisical vision. Issued paperbound. The poet found the cover image, a landscape ("Untitled #281) painting by Joan Nelson.

JOHN BALABAN
Words for My Daughter
Selecting this book for publication in the National Poetry Series, W.S. Merwin wrote, "From the beginning, Balaban's gift for language has been wholly devoted to his need to face directly and mine sense from the bewilderment and anguish of being implicated in the history and suffering of our time." A conscientious objector during the Vietnam War, Balaban considers clarifying moments of love, virtue, and memories of war – Dante's "proper subjects for poetry" – while hitchhiking alone in the vast deserts of the American Southwest. Maxine Kumin observed, "These stunning and courageous poems haunt us with their compassion. Balaban is the master of juxtapositions." The poet is also a masterful translator of Vietnamese poetry. Issued paperbound.

Pablo Neruda
The Book of Questions
The sixth and concluding volume from translator William O'Daly is exactly what the title suggests: a book composed entirely of (mostly unanswerable, in the conventional sense) enigmatic questions. In these poems the sacred and the profane become the Janus masks of the world, reality defined in the margins of a silence molded by encounters between the taken-for-granted things of daily experience and the boundless imagination of one of this century's greatest poets. O'Daly's saintly devotion to Neruda's poetry spanned seventeen years, presenting the elderly poet at the height of his ineffable powers in seamless, nearly transparent translations. Published in cloth and paperbound editions. Galen Garwood's covers for this series are among my favorites.

ᝫ 1992

Stephen Berg
New and Selected Poems
W.S. Merwin remarked on this book, "Stephen Berg is a poet (and translator and editor) of such energy, range, intimacy, daring, narrative and evocative authority, that it is hard to understand why his work has not received a wide welcome long before this. I hope the present selection will be the occasion for changing all that." Berg's *Selected Poems* also comes with ringing praise from Denise Levertov, Kenneth Rexroth, Hayden Carruth, C.K. Williams and William Arrowsmith. The *New York Times* named this book one of the year's ten best. Published in cloth and paperbound editions.

Sandor Csoóri
Selected Poems
A generous selection of poems spanning the career of the leading Hungarian poet of the post–World War II generation. His poems, at once public and private, have made him the conscience and teacher of his country, a chronicler of the vast tragedies and small triumphs of his people. He is also a remarkable love poet. Translated, with native-speaking collaborators, by a very fine poet, Len Roberts. Published paperbound.

Hayden Carruth
Collected Shorter Poems, 1946–1991
Winner of the National Book Critics Circle Award and finalist for the National

Book Award, this first half of Carruth's two-volume *Collected Poems* collects more than 400 pages of the poet's best shorter work. Galway Kinnell remarked, "This is not a man who sits down to 'write a poem'; rather, some burden of understanding and feeling, some need to *know*, forces his poems into being." Adrienne Rich called his work a "part of our country's poetic treasure." Published in cloth and paperbound editions, Swenson's cover is appropriately totemic. This is a book to go to school on.

David Romtvedt
A Flower Whose Name I Do Not Know
Selecting this, the poet's third collection of poetry, for publication in the National Poetry Series, John Haines observed, "David Romtvedt is a fine poet and an honest man... I have learned much from reading these poems, and have found additional satisfaction in listening to a voice from a part of our continent (rural Wyoming) not often heard from." Romtvedt is distinguished by, among other things, refusing to sign a loyalty oath at the University of Southwestern Louisiana. His poems address a profound commitment to social and environmental responsibility. Published paperbound.

Michael White
The Island
This book came by way of Mark Strand, then serving as Poet Laureate, who also found special funding to·make publication possible and who wrote, "No first book in recent memory has so much wisdom, so much lyric conviction as Michael White's *The Island*. I find his poems astonishingly mature, profound, evocative." Richard Howard called this "a book of grand and luminous peregrinations." Issued paperbound.

↶ 1993

W. S. Merwin
The Second Four Books of Poems
The Second Four Books includes all the poetry of *The Lice* (1963), *The Moving Target* (1967), *The Carrier of Ladders* (1970, and for which Merwin received the Pulitzer Prize), and *Writings to an Unfinished Accompaniment* (1973) – some of the most startlingly original and influential poetry of the second half of this century, moving, as Richard Howard wrote, "from preterition to presence to prophecy." Writing in 1970, Adrienne Rich said, "Merwin's new poems are more open than ever in their account of human loneliness and the miracles of the revelation that

happen in spite of it. They reach backward and forward as he connects himself with the archaic, the totemic, the legendary, yet exists on the verge of our shattering future." Issued paperbound.

LUCILLE CLIFTON
The Book of Light
Clifton's *Book of Light,* with a striking painting by Jody Kim on the cover, is among our all-time bestsellers. Begging "the divine to speak," Clifton discovers "the stillness that is god," bearing witness to a wonderful poet's awe and gratitude for a world of passionate discovery, humane anger, and rich devotion. Published in cloth and paperbound editions.

XAVIER VILLAURRUTIA
Nostalgia for Death
Villaurrutia was one of the very few Latin American writers in the first half of this century who was openly homosexual, an important Mexican poet who wrote essentially one book, translated here for the first time by Eliot Weinberger. This edition includes a book-length essay by Octavio Paz (translated by Esther Allen), *Hieroglyphs of Desire,* in which he says Villaurrutia "discovered that there are secret corridors running between dreaming and wakefulness, love and hate, absence and presence. The best of his work is an exploration of these corridors... The poetry of Villaurrutia seems to have been written not only in some other country, but in a place beyond geography and history, beyond myth and legend, a nowhere that 'occupies no place in space,' in which time has stopped." Published paperbound, the astonishing cover photo is by Gerardo Suter.

SHIRLEY KAUFMAN
Rivers of Salt
The poems of Kaufman's sixth collection, cross geographical and cultural boundaries – Seattle to Jerusalem, the Dead Sea to Lago di Como. Many of her poems record a life in Israel that has deepened her awareness and added historical weight to her response in days haunted by longing, vulnerable to war and the fear and suffering that is its inevitable consequence. She finds "that which flickers as joy in the middle of grieving." Her first book with Copper Canyon Press was published paperbound incorporating a painting by a wonderful Israeli landscape painter, Ruth Levin.

TERRY EHRET
Lost Body
Terry Ehret's first book was selected for publication in the National Poetry Series by Carolyn Kizer, who enthused, "I salute her achievement. Her poems are one

more step for womankind." The poems explore her sense of estrangement from needs and desires, and often from her own body as she struggles for identity and definition and the continual recreation of self in intimacy, in motherhood and in language. Published paperbound.

JANE MILLER
August Zero
Against an end-of-the-century scenario filled with the threats of population explosion and environmental disaster, Miller describes a post-apocalyptic resurrection of consciousness in poems with jarring juxtapositions, metaphors, associative and dissociative reflections, myth, and dream. This book, her fourth major collection of poetry, received the Western States Book Award. Published in cloth and paperbound editions, the cover image, "Shore Birds in NYC" by Jacqueline Hayden, is memorable.

T'AO CH'IEN
Selected Poems
Also known as T'ao Yuan-Ming (365–427 CE), T'ao Ch'ien was the first writer to make poetry based upon his natural voice and immediate experience. He has come to hold a quasi-mythic status for his commitment to a reclusive farm life, accepting poverty and other hardships, writing poetry that mirrors the lived life. He is the grandfather of Chinese poetry, and David Hinton's translations are, in the words of Burton Watson, "varied and imaginative while remaining faithful." Published paperbound.

CAROLYN KIZER
Proses: On Poems & Poets
The inaugural volume in the *Writing Re: Writing* series collects essays and reviews by the Pulitzer Prize winning poet. She offers the first major American appreciation of the English poet John Clare, discusses the influence of Pope on her own poetry, and assays a variety of poets including Hayden Carruth, Denise Levertov, Louise Bogan, Robert Creeley, John Berryman, Marge Piercy and others, as well as a major autobiographical essay. Cover painting by Richard Diebenkorn. The *Writing Re: Writing Series* was begun because we felt there was a need for good books on poetry by leading poets, books for a general readership as much as for the scholarly community. Books in this series are published in paperbound editions.

ᔕ 1994

HAYDEN CARRUTH
Collected Longer Poems
For fifty years, Carruth's poetry has been distinguished by the indelible presence
of passion, compassion, and radical philosophy. His renowned technical genius is
perfectly matched to his ear for regional idiom and narrative structure. His *Longer
Poems* includes poems in sequence, and meditative and narrative poems that have
made him the most accessible "regional" poet since Robert Frost. Publication of
his two-volume *Collected Poems* ranks among our finest achievements at the
Press. Published in cloth and paperbound editions. John Berry's first book design
for the press was created to pair with Tree Swenson's design for *Collected Shorter
Poems*.

MARVIN BELL
The Book of the Dead Man
Bell's ninth major collection of poems is groundbreaking, his most provocative
and imaginative to date. The phrase "the dead man" resounds like a drumbeat reg-
istering the wisdom and genius of ignorance, fallibility, and mutability with a
Zen-like detachment. These poems demand to be understood in the context of
the incantatory line as it demolishes boundaries between lyric poetry and serio-
comic intensity, between spiritual candor and common desire. Published in cloth
and paperbound editions with Garwood's astonishing monotype "Anubis" on the
cover.

SU TUNG-P'O
Selected Poems
One of the greatest poets in China's long literary history, Su lived during the Sung
dynasty in the eleventh century. Falling into disfavor with the imperial court, he
served time in jail and was exiled to the island of Hainan. Permitted to return to
the mainland, he turned to farming, studying with a Zen master and roaming the
mountains and rivers. Gary Snyder wrote of this book, "Burton Watson is the fin-
est, most consistent, most generous translator of Chinese literature of this century
… [His] splendid translation is a real gift. Su Tung-p'o's elegant, diverse poems are
full of compassion, vision, the sense of the moment, the sweetness and hardness
of life. What a joy to meet his bright, undefeated spirit." This winner of the PEN
Translation Prize was published paperbound. In the midst of production, a
printer's error resulted in altering the original design, a "mistake" we chose to re-
tain.

CYRUS CASSELLS
Soul Make a Path Through Shouting
The second book by a poet whose first book (*The Mud Actor*, 1982) was selected for publication in the National Poetry Series by Al Young, *Soul* is his first with Copper Canyon Press. Rita Dove called this "The most spectacular book I've seen in years. Not only are the poems enthralling – they are heartfelt, with that largeness of spirit found in great literature, possessing a vision that embraces and enriches. Cassells is one of the most exciting poets writing in the United States today." Published in cloth and paperbound editions, the cover painting by Barbara Thomas – a landscape with burning book, the painting in the shape of a crow – is just right.

KAREN SWENSON
The Landlady in Bangkok
Selected for publication in the National Poetry Series by Maxine Kumin, Swenson's third book of poems, her first with Copper Canyon Press, chronicles her journeys in Southern Asia, exposing moral ambiguities where cultures clash and where the human population devastates the natural environment. With remarkable technical dexterity, she searches beneath the surface of politics and philosophy to reveal essential human character. Issued paperbound with a most amazing Buddha on the cover.

RICHARD JONES
A Perfect Time
In his third book of poems (and third with Copper Canyon Press), Jones invokes the essential joy, suffering, and spiritual awakening of the attentive life. He writes with a deceptive simplicity, honing his narrative skills to arrive at a poetry made luminous by parable-like, aphoristic wisdom. I risk redundancy but this is another brilliant image, a painting from Galen Garwood, this one in some way rhyming with Joan Nelson's landscape on Jones's *Paradise*. Published paperbound.

OLGA BROUMAS & T BEGLEY
Sappho's Gymnasium
Returning us to the traditions of two great Greek lyric poets, Sappho (sixth century BCE) and 1979 Nobel Laureate Odysseas Elytis, *Sappho's Gymnasium* presents the collaborative act at its most intensely lyrical pitch. Sustained by the oral ecstatic tradition, here poetry is an issue of the body, and the body is the instrument of poetry. The result is a seamless intoxicating music. Jane Miller observed, "Broumas and Begley have resuscitated the Sapphic lyric to serve the holy and ho-

listic in the next millennium, and we are better 'sacred idiots' for it. I read these
poems trembling." Published paperbound, the cover image is by Broumas and
Begley.

ᗐ 1995

DAVID BOTTOMS
Armored Hearts: Selected & New Poems
Joining a generous collection of new poems to those selected from four previous
award-winning volumes, *Armored Hearts* presents the power of idiomatic narra-
tive at its naked best. Louis Simpson wrote of this book, "Bottoms transforms the
experiences of the individual into poetry that speaks eloquently of the human
condition. These scenes and incidents are rendered in unforgettable detail." Pub-
lished in cloth and paperbound editions with a painting of a devastated landscape
by former Southern, recent Northwest, painter Paul Harcharik.

JAMES GALVIN
Lethal Frequencies
Firsthand knowledge of the expansive landscape of the Rocky Mountain West
provides perspective more than mere imagery, reducing human activity to its
proper dimension in Galvin's fourth collection. He brings a kind of pre-Socratic
intelligence, a stoical turn of mind, and genuine love of hard physical work to
make poems that are direct, spare to the point of being terse, stripped of rhetorical
or aesthetic device. Published paperbound, cover painting by Beverly Pepper.

ERIN BELIEU
Infanta
The poet's first book, *Infanta* was selected for publication in the National Poetry
Series by Hayden Carruth, who wrote, "The poems have a sophisticated urban
chic that is both attractive and deceptive. Beneath their verbal glamour, which is
considerable, they embody an intelligence both sensual and political. They speak
to the beleaguered outposts of compassion in our society. They are original, fresh,
extraordinarily skillful, grounded at the same time in literary, including historical,
awareness and humane contemporary concern." Published paperbound; cover
painting, Catherine Paciotti's "Laocöon," suggested by the poet. Named among
the *Washington Post's* "Best Books of the Year."

DAVID LEE
My Town
In naming this book winner of the Western States Book Award, the judges cited
Lee's search "for the soul of a small town, where everybody knows when you
flounder or fall." Hayden Carruth added, "Country speech is the same all over, or
nearly. David Lee's farmerfolk in Utah speak the same idioms and rhythms I've
know in Vermont, and his ear catches the nuances exactly, beautifully. It's a speech
full of eloquence, pathos, and humor, full of music, full of good sense. I could read
it all week." Issued paperbound with a great cover image from a wood engraving
(by Gaylord Schanilec) of a three-legged dog in a small town. Yammy. Like the
rich yammy orange of Wingate sandstone near Lee's home in St. George, Utah.

ODYSSEAS ELYTIS
Open Papers: Selected Essays
Open Papers is the primary statement on his art by the recipient of the 1979 Nobel
Prize in Literature, a sweeping exploration of the mind and mythic imagination of
one of the most original, visionary, and compelling poets of this century. In part
autobiographical, it also chronicles the life of poetry in modern Greece, especially
as regards the profound influence of surrealism. His essays, like his poetry, sparkle
with numinous discovery and a passionate commitment to art – "the second con-
dition of the world" – as a living process. From many hands comes this singular
voice, including editorial assistance and dealing with extraordinary design prob-
lems including multiple languages, the translation itself funded in part by the
Witter Bynner Foundation. Paperbound.

ARTHUR SZE
Archipelago
By turns spiritual and imaginative, meditative and active, Sze's poems in *Archi-
pelago* are inspired in part by the famous Zen garden at Ryoanji where fifteen
stones are set in a sea of raked gravel and each stone – or in this case, each poem –
is seen only within the context of a larger interdependence. Imbued with the spirit
of Zen, *Archipelago* harnesses the power of silence in order to reveal what Chuang
Tzu called, "the third unspoken thing," the unnameable that binds imaginative
and physical worlds. I had admired Sze's poems and translations from classical
Chinese – most notably his translations of Tu Fu, whom I have also translated –
for years. Issued paperbound. Cover photo of the garden at Ryoanji is by writer
and Asian art scholar Stephen Addiss.

TIMOTHY LIU
Burnt Offerings
The second book by a gay Chinese-American poet who turned to poetry in part
as a result of his frustration with the Mormon Church, at whose service he was a
missionary in Hong Kong. Marilyn Hacker called him, "a poet of *eros* in all guises,
from acts performed defiantly, worshipfully, in public toilet stalls to the intricate
dance of the senses and spirit that is two men's loving, or losing each other. His
eros is *agape* also, a love-feast for his readers as it modulates through loss to a cel-
ebration of the numinous quotidian, the precisely graceful details through which
memories and histories survive." Issued paperbound. The cover painting by
Leonard Baskin was suggested by the author; I had followed Baskin's work for
years – ever since publication of Ted Hughes's *Crow*.

KORIYAMA NAOSHI AND EDWARD LUEDERS, EDITORS & TRANSLATORS
Like Underground Water: The Poetry of Mid-Twentieth Century Japan
With more than 240 poems by eighty-one poets, this is the first comprehensive
anthology of post–World War II Japanese poetry to survey all the major tenden-
cies and developments in poetry directly influenced by the war. Naomi Shihab
Nye has called this book "one of the most important poetry anthologies of the last
decade of the twentieth century…we have needed much more than haiku, and
here it is… Gratitude to Koriyama and Lueders for an enormous task well done,
and for the honor we readers now share of understanding more deeply the poetic
soul of Japan." Published in cloth and paperbound editions. I selected the cover
image ("Siltri I") by John-Franklin Koenig, who divides his time been Seattle and
France.

THOMAS CENTOLELLA
Lights & Mysteries
The poet's second book and second with Copper Canyon Press. Denise Levertov
(who selected his *Terra Firma* for publication in the 1990 National Poetry Series)
wrote of this book, "This is an exciting book – so much passion, compassion, hu-
mor, zest for living, sadness, and big questions. The amplitude of Centolella's
forms allows for a rare synthesis of meditative discourse and lyrical sensibility,
and the personal yet shareable vision which informed his first book is intensified
in the greater maturity of this new collection. Issued paperbound. Cover art is by
Gray Foster.

ELAINE TERRANOVA
Damages
The second book by the previous winner of the Walt Whitman award, chronicles,
as Colette Inez has written, "the body's betrayals, childhood's tortured paths and

restless journeys, the danger inside the seemingly commonplace events of our comings and goings. Elegant metaphors and sure-footed cadences dazzle as the poet guides us through her dark crosscuts and interstices. Subtle as oracles and as demanding of respect, Terranova's fearless poems call for our wonder and admiration." Published paperbound. The cover image, suggested by the poet, is by Carole Sivin.

↜ 1996

HAYDEN CARRUTH
Selected Essays & Reviews
Another monumental book, this one collecting Carruth's essays and reviews on poetry. In an unusually enthusiastic review, *Publishers Weekly* observed, "This is impassioned poetry criticism of the best sort. So good, in fact, that even those without a taste for poetry (or for criticism, for that matter) will find themselves entertained and instructed... Carruth's most valuable contribution is not only context but real style and years of thinking about the more transcendental subjects of poetry." Carruth is the most lucid and honest and unflinching critic of poetry in our time. Published paperbound, the third volume in our *Writing Re: Writing Series*. The cover image, suggested by the poet, is a view of my front garden at Kage-an from the chair where he took morning coffee during a visit; photo by my wife, Gray Foster.

ANNA SWIR
Talking to My Body
Translated and Introduced by Nobel Laureate Czeslaw Milosz and Leonard Nathan, these terse, unsparing and unsentimentally direct poems describe the erotic life of the poet's body – its appetites and hungers, its losses and births and longings. Born in Warsaw in the first decade of this century, Anna Swir's first poems were published in the 1930s, and she shared in the fate of Warsaw during the Nazi siege. She is modern Poland's preeminent feminist poet. She observed, "The poet should be as sensitive as an aching tooth." Published paperbound with a striking cover image provided by sculptor Stephanie Lutgring.

HAYDEN CARRUTH
Scrambled Eggs and Whiskey: Poems 1991–1995
Anna Swir was in her sixties when she mastered the poetics of Eros; Carruth, now in his seventies, has long been a master of the erotic poem, but with this book he

has written mature love poetry that rivals the late great work of William Carlos Williams and Rexroth. Along with the splendid erotic poems, Carruth's sequential homage to Tu Fu, his poems dealing with his daughter's struggle with cancer, and a dazzling poem addressed to Marilyn Hacker show him to be at the pinnacle of his powers. Published in cloth and paperbound editions.

SHIRLEY KAUFMAN
Roots in the Air: New and Selected Poems
A generous selection from this poet-translator's six previous volumes together with new poems, *Roots in the Air* offers ample opportunity to assay the major work of this American poet living in Israel. Sandra Gilbert calls her "a poet of suave understatement, poignant lucidity, extraordinarily telling detail. To these qualities [she has] added what has long been gathering in her work: the terrible and powerful maturity of a woman who knows that we have all been forced by history into (as the title of one of her strongest poems puts it) 'Looking for Prophets.'" Published paperbound. The cover painting is by Guy Anderson, whose work I've admired for many years.

EMILY WARN
The Novice Insomniac
The second book by the poet and the second published (paperbound) by Copper Canyon Press appears nearly fourteen years after her first, *The Leaf Path*. Her sense of craft has deepened as her vision has matured in poems drawing from the Talmudic tradition as well as from years of studying wilderness areas of the Pacific Northwest. Her personal modesty and commitment to artistic integrity shine throughout her work. The cover painting is by Laura K. Popenoe.

HEATHER ALLEN
Leaving a Shadow
When Denise Levertov selected this book for publication in the National Poetry Series, we had a wonderful conversation about whether the poet was male or female. Neither of us could be certain. How refreshing! Levertov noted how Allen's work "contrasts sharply with the current craze for narcissistic exhibitionism, but these poems are by no means impersonal... Allen writes out of a fully lived (and evidently long, and long-remembered, and *re*lived) experience of lake and forest, with their light and darkness, silence and sounds, stillness and movement; their deer, crows, owls, solitary fishermen; their ongoing secret life." Published paperbound. The cover photo is by Alan Wiener.

CAROLYN KIZER
Harping On: Poems 1985–1995
Ten years of new poems are gathered here by the Pulitzer Prize winner, including major new long poems and her memorable and often political light verse. A feminist long before the word entered the contemporary lexicon, whether writing formal or improvisational verse, there is simply no one like her. The cover image is by Salvatore Federico and was painted specifically for this book, published in cloth and paperbound editions.

JANE MILLER
Memory at These Speeds: New and Selected Poems
When Miller received the Western States Book Award, the judges cited her "skillful, irrepressible imagination," noting how she "sustained vision and intelligence from beginning to end." I hasten to add that she also has an ear that is nonpareil. Marilyn Hacker notes her "jazzy sensual line that creates the illusion of improvisation but never loses the accretive power of narrative or sensory evocation." Miller is a post-punk *bête noire* oracle for the *fin de mundo* of "the American century." The author found the cover image, a manipulated Polaroid photograph by Patrick Nagatani. Paperbound.

W. S. MERWIN
Flower & Hand
All the poems from *The Compass Flower* and *The Opening of the Hand* with the suite "Feathers from the Hill" in a single paperbound volume. Our second major collection from this remarkable poet, one of the most luminous, distinguished and influential voices in American poetry in the last half of this century. He has earned his voluminous awards. And more. Not only for his poetry, but for his translations from several languages, for his prose, and for the model he has set for all the poets who follow.

YUAN MEI
I Don't Bow to Buddhas: Selected Poems
J. P. Seaton's seamless translations of the last great poet (1716–1798) of the classical Chinese tradition. A religious skeptic, Confucian classics scholar, feminist and gourmet food writer, Yuan Mei was nonetheless profoundly influenced by *ch'an*. In his biography of the poet, Arthur Waley notes, "The one aspect (apart from his genius as a writer) in which Yuan Mei seems to have been unique was his persistence, despite the advice of friends, in publishing writings of a sort that other authors suppressed. It was thought clownish and undignified to print humorous poems, and improper to print references to concubines, young actors, and so on." The cover image is a portrait of Bodhidarma, who also didn't bow to Buddhas. Paperbound.

SAM HAMILL, EDITOR
The Gift of Tongues
The cover image is from a copper mask by George Tsutakawa. The year I spent editing this tome, including work from forthcoming books through 1997, our twenty-fifth year, I witnessed the potential demise of the National Endowment for the Arts and the prospect of loss of major support from private foundations. I hope I haven't spent a year engraving a Copper Canyon Press tombstone. Published in cloth and paperbound editions. As Thales remarked, "They have hope who have nothing else."

↶ 1997

STEPHEN BERG
The Steel Cricket: Versions, 1958-1996
Following in the tradition of Ezra Pound's reinvention of Sextus Propertius, Stephen Berg has for many years reinvented the diverse poetry of, among others, Ikkyu (see *Crow with No Mouth* under 1989), Anna Akhmatova (see under *New & Selected Poems*), Miklos Radnoti, Eskimo songs, Antonio Machado, Aztec songs, and others. Kenneth Rexroth wrote of Berg's versions of Akhmatova, "The only word for the Akhmatova poems is amazing.... Berg has done a magnificent job of 'method' – completely projecting himself into another person." The late William Arrowsmith compared him to Whitman, Pavese, and James Wright. This book collects (paperbound) all of Berg's major "versions of poems" other than Ikkyu and Akhmatova, which remains separately in print.

SUNG IL-LEE, TRANSLATOR
The Moonlit Pond: Korean Classical Poems in Chinese
Like the Japanese and other East Asian cultures, classical Korean poets wrote one kind of poetry in Korean, another in classical Chinese. This is the first major anthology to assay the Chinese-style poems of a long and lively lyrical tradition reaching from the mid-ninth century to the twentieth.

SUSAN GRIFFIN
Collected Poems
This major collection of poetry spans a writing career that has also included several of the most important works of nonfiction in our time: *The Eros of Everyday Life, Pornography and Silence, Woman and Nature,* and *A Chorus of Stones: The Life of War.* Marge Piercy has noted that Griffin's poems are "extremely readable

and compelling" as the poet struggles "to connect us across the generations and across species, to place us where we belong in a web of social caring inside nature, nurtured and nurturing, but these poems never forget the forces and odds against such tenderness."

ELEANOR WILNER
New and Selected Poems

I have been a devoted admirer of Eleanor Wilner's poetry for many years, since her first book, *Maya,* was published by the University of Massachusetts Press in 1979. But despite a MacArthur Fellowship and many other honors, her poetry has not been widely reviewed. This major collection will, I hope, bring her the broad readership she so richly deserves. Highly allusive, wise beyond years, and with an ear for the line that is utterly captivating, Wilner is one of the best poets writing today.

CYRUS CASSELLS
Beautiful Signor

This is the third book (his second by Copper Canyon Press) of this major new voice from the gay community. This book, more personal in tone perhaps than his universally praised *Soul Make a Path Through Shouting,* forms a kind of contemporary *Song of Songs,* celebrating unwavering tenderness in poems written almost entirely on travels in Europe. Slightly baroque, highly musical, they include the poet's meditations on history and religion as they filter through the pilgrim's lens.

JOHN HAINES
Poems 1948–1953

I've known John Haines and admired his poetry and essays for more than twenty years and included an appreciative essay on his work in my *A Poet's Work.* When he sent me a copy of a limited edition chapbook from Limberlost Press (*Where the Twilight Never Ends*) and I read a sampling of his early poems – poems influenced in part by Chinese poetry in translation – I suggested a small volume from his earliest work, poems not included in previous books. The result provides a great introductory view of Haines as a young poet in New York, Provincetown, and in the Carmel Valley. Paperbound.

ODYSSEAS ELYTIS
Selected & Last Poems

Translated by Olga Broumas. One of the last acts of the poet – literally hours before his death on the last day of winter, 1996 – was to put together a packet of his last poems for his friend and translator Olga Broumas. This volume collects her previous translations, including *What I Love* and *The Little Mariner*, together with translations of Elytis's last poems. Famous for his descriptions of Greek light, his friends knew him as The Owl who wrote all night. The Owl is gone, but his fire is bright.

JOHN BALABAN
New and Selected Poems
A generous selection of poems spanning more than twenty-five years, this volume demonstrates Balaban's technical virtuosity as well as his uncanny ability to find the personal in the political, the political in the personal, all while maintaining an honestly compassionate perspective. Denise Levertov wrote of his first book, *After Our War* (1974), "Probably the best writing by an American to have emerged from direct encounter with the horror of that [Vietnam] war." In the years since, his poetry has continued to reveal a deep personal sense of responsibility in his engagement with history, family, and locale.

JAMES GALVIN
Resurrection Update: New and Collected Poems
This major collection gathers poems from more than a quarter century of acclaimed writing. Spare, often stoical, James Galvin is clear-headed and elemental like a modern-day Herakleitos or some Taoist sage speaking from time's farthest hermitage. Like a mouthful of fresh fallen snow, his poems sometimes include an ache in the teeth. The harsh sub-rural landscapes of southwestern Wyoming often provide a perspective for Galvin, placing human endeavor in its proper dimension, revealing a poetry of mature disciplined vision stripped of mere artifice or academic wit. – "The world is not / your philosophical problem." Which of course it is. Isn't it?

THOMAS MCGRATH
Letter to an Imaginary Friend
Published nearly ten years after the poet's death in 1988, this is the complete, definitive edition of the poem Diane Wakoski called "the first great poem out of the heart of the American Midwest." Thirty years in the writing, *Letter* is an Odyssean journey accomplished with great complexity while remaining the most enjoyably *readable* major poem of our time. McGrath draws upon Hopi mythology, revolutionary working class devotions, flashbacks and flash-forwards, juxtapositions (Lisbon, Portugal, with Lisbon, North Dakota, among many), and great lyrical passages to weave his magic. Philip Levine has written: "I hope I can someday give this country or the few poetry lovers of this country something as large, soulful, honest and beautiful as McGrath's great and still unappreciated epic of our mad

and lyric century, *Letter to an Imaginary Friend,* a book from which we can draw hope and sustenance for as long as we last."

1998

ARTHUR SZE
The Redshifting Web: Poems 1970–1996
This major collection from the author of *Archipelago,* winner of an American Book Award in 1996, includes major work from each of his five previous books along with new poems. Quincy Troupe said it best: "Arthur Sze composes an elegant, quietly intense, very human, beautiful poetry, one that is remarkable for its commitment to metaphor and musical language. I consider him one of the foremost poets of his generation. He is wise, intelligent, a joy to be with and read."

MARVIN BELL
Ardor (The Book of the Dead Man, Volume Two, 34–70)
The author writes in his Preface, "The Dead Man is not a persona, not a mask. He is not me alone, for that would be an insufficient measure. He is the one who does not turn on a lamp to study the dark, but is himself the lantern." The Dead Man stands conventional wisdom and syntax on their heads and laughs at Herakleitos for not standing firm in the middle of the river, and at Chuang Tzu for wanting it both ways at once. In this he is like the politician who speaks of himself in the third person. Don't be fooled. The Dead Man is alive and kicking.

A Note on the Editor

SAM HAMILL has published a dozen volumes of original poetry, most recently *Destination Zero: Poems 1970-1995* (White Pine Press, 1995). He has also published more than a dozen volumes of poetry translated from ancient Greek, Chinese, Japanese, and Latin, and three volumes of essays. His anthology exploring thirty centuries of erotic poetry, *The Erotic Spirit*, is published by Shambhala. He has been the recipient of fellowships from the National Endowment for the Arts, the Guggenheim Foundation, the U.S.–Japan Friendship Commission, the Lila Wallace–Readers Digest Fund and the Andrew F. Mellon Foundation. He is Contributing Editor at *Tricycle: The Buddhist Review* and at *The American Poetry Review*.

Book design and composition by John D. Berry, Jennifer Van West, and Sam Hamill, using Adobe Pagemaker 6.0 and a Power Computing 120. The typeface is Minion multiple master, designed by Robert Slimbach as part of the Adobe Originals type library. Minion is based on typefaces of the later Renaissance, but is derived from no single source. Slimbach designed Minion in 1990, then expanded it in 1992 to become a multiple master font – the first to include a size axis for optical scaling. *Printed by McNaughton & Gunn.*

DISCARDED

811.5408 G366g 1996

The gift of tongues :
twenty-five years of

Library
Western Wyoming Community College

DEMCO